BASIC CHRISTIAN BELIEFS

BASIC CHRISTIAN BELIEFS

FREDERICK C. GRANT

OLIVER AND BOYD

EDINBURGH AND LONDON

OLIVER AND BOYD LTD
Tweeddale Court
Edinburgh 1

39A Welbeck Street
London, W.1

Unless otherwise noted, the quotations from the Bible
are from the Revised Standard Version. B.C.P. means
the version in the Book of Common Prayer; and A.R.V.
the American Revised Version (1901).

FIRST PUBLISHED 1960

PRINTED IN GREAT BRITAIN
BY ROBERT CUNNINGHAM AND SONS LTD, ALVA

Contents

5

To The Most Reverend
PHILIP CARRINGTON, D.D.
ARCHBISHOP OF QUEBEC
with gratitude for
Thirty Years of Friendship

1

Christianity and Other Religions

Our Basic Beliefs

THE basic Christian beliefs are those which provide the foundation of the whole Christian view of life. They determine what we Christians think about the world we live in, about other persons, and about our own duties and responsibilities in this life. They also determine what Christians think about the life to come—that is, man's nature and man's destiny. There are, of course, a number of Christian beliefs which are not really basic, but depend upon the other and more fundamental beliefs. For example, the nature of the angels, or the precise degree of divine inspiration in the Bible (i.e. whether it is "verbal" or not)—these are really secondary beliefs, or, as we say, beliefs "not necessary to salvation".

Among the really basic beliefs the first and most important is *belief in God*. This means not only the belief that God exists (which probably most persons hold in one form or other), but the belief that God is the Creator of the world, the Final Judge of all mankind, the One whose wisdom, goodness, and love sustain all things; who has taken the initiative in revealing Himself to men, and has told us what His purposes are, and what He requires of those who would serve Him; who sent "prophets and wise men" to declare His will, and finally sent His own Son to be the Saviour of all who believe in Him and follow His way of life. One may therefore say that the Christian belief in God underlies all other Christian beliefs and

7

teachings, and forms the foundation upon which they rest. Without this central, fundamental belief, the other beliefs would hang in midair—like the houses built from the ridge-pole downward, in Dean Swift's *Gulliver's Travels*.

It is also the belief by which all other beliefs must be tested. If they turn out to be inconsistent with the Christian belief in God (i.e. with belief in the character of God as revealed in Christ), then they cannot be viewed as Christian beliefs, and must be given up. Or if they require an idea of God which is contrary to the Christian, they must be discarded. There have been various theological systems, in the past, some of them widely influential, which presupposed ideas of God which in time proved to be incompatible with the basic conception set forth in the Gospel; and so they had to be abandoned. The test of any new doctrine must always be: What does it do to our belief in God? If it represents God as harsh, vindictive, stupid, cruel—merely a magnified man and a barbarian at that—then we cannot accept it.

Moreover, it is the belief in God by which Christianity must be tested and compared with other religions. The idea that all religions are alike, or that all the modern world needs is "more religion", or that all religions are only "more or less true, more or less false"—such ideas are badly out of focus, and fail to make clear the essential character of either Christianity or any of its rivals. Despite some real and striking resemblances, there is a world of difference between Buddhism, Islam, and Christianity. These differences make it impossible to say "Hinduism for the Hindus, Islam for the Arabs, and Christianity for us". There is really, one suspects, a note of contempt in such a sweeping rejection of Christian missions—it is not far removed from saying, "The other religions are good enough for their adherents; why bother to offer them another?" If the human race is essentially one—which is certainly the assumption of all modern biologists,

8

anthropologists, and historians—then there must be one religion which is the best for all mankind. There are not different astronomies or chemistries or sciences of medicine suitable for the various races of mankind; there is only *one true* astronomy, *one true* system of chemistry, *one true* science of medicine, and so on.

Since comparison—and competition—is inevitable, the question comes down to this: Which is the true belief in God? Which belief in God best—i.e., most truly—reflects God as He really is? Which revelation of God is the full, final, complete revelation? To this full revelation the other faiths were no doubt preparatory, as stages in an on-going process of divine revelation; but this one is final, in the sense that nothing more can be added, for it is the fullest revelation possible under the terms and conditions of our human life in this present world. This revelation, we Christians believe, was completed in Christ: i.e., He took for granted and built upon the preceding stages in the age-old course of divine communication, and carried the revelation to its full development.[1]

What the New Testament affirmed of the Old Testament Law and Prophets, as preparatory to the teaching of Christ and to Christian belief about Him, was applied by the later Church to the religions and the culture of the world outside Palestine. Greek philosophy, Roman law, Jewish religion—these three together formed the *praeparatio evangelica*, "the preparation for the Gospel", according to the Church Fathers. They were the "three measures of meal" into which was stirred the leaven of the Gospel (Lk. XIII.21). The principle could also be applied to the pagan religions, which reflected, some more clearly, some less, the deep yearnings of men for "life, a more abundant

---

[1] See Mt. v.17f; Acts x.34-35; Jn. 1.9; Heb. 1.1-4. The obscure saying in Jn. x.8, "All who came before me are thieves and robbers", may refer to the numerous false Messianic claimants in first-century Palestine, so that it does not contradict the other texts just cited.

life," and for a trustworthy and indubitable self-revelation by God Himself in human language and in a human person. One need not try to prove all other religions false; they were only incomplete, preparatory. Nor need we claim that Christianity—the actual, empirical religion of the Christian Church—is perfect, while all other religions are imperfect; for we Christians have not yet measured up to the standard of our "high calling of God in Christ Jesus" (Phil. III.14, A.V.), and others who "enter into our labours" (Jn. IV.38) may produce a far richer harvest than we. It is quite conceivable that Indian, Chinese, or Japanese Christianity may some day outstrip the European-American types in the full realisation of God's promises in the Gospel. Finally, it is quite unnecessary—and really impossible—to describe Christianity as "not a religion, but a divine, supernatural life in grace, which can only be contrasted with the world's so-called 'religions'." This is not the way the New Testament and the early Church conceived of Christianity (see, e.g., Acts XVII.23, XXIV.13). Other conceptions of God were not looked upon as false, but only as partial.

> They are but broken lights of thee,
> And thou, O Lord, art more than they.

Christianity and the Ancient Religions

Never, apparently, has there been a people wholly devoid of religion. The earliest traces of human culture, even as early as the Old Stone Age, seem to reflect religious ideas of one kind or another. We cannot say that man has always been religious, or that "primitive" men worshipped God—for we do not know anything about "primitive" men. Men may perhaps have been living on this planet 300,000 years ago. But by "primitive" we usually mean only "prehistoric"; and it is clearly true that prehistoric men were religious, i.e. they recognised powers outside or above themselves to which serious attention must be paid. All of the great historic religions of the Ancient World preserve traits inherited from pre-history, especially in their cults (or ritual), their holy places, the names of divine beings, and even, very often, in the barbarous myths that were still told, revised, and explained as sacred tales. These "primitive" survivals in the ancient religions point clearly to a long pre-history, whose records no longer exist (if records ever existed, even orally) and hence cannot provide the meanings of their many surviving rites—if ever they had any consistent, rational meaning.

Basically, the historical religions of the Ancient World seem to rest upon a foundation of *animism*, i.e. the belief that certain things, places, persons, or physical phenomena are essentially supernatural, and are either identical with, or contain, supernormal powers (perhaps demonic) which may either blast and destroy or bless and enrich those who come in contact with them. Some historians of religion have distinguished a "pre-deistic" period when people believed only in local powers (*numina*), not gods; but the difference was partly one of definition. An African savage may worship his amulet or ritual mask; on the other hand, the poet Horace could refer to the *numen* presiding over the cool spring on his little farm as the lovely gentle goddess Bandusia. This level of pre-historic animism, surviving as a substratum beneath all the ancient historical religions, was characterised by two great basic beliefs which produced their two most fundamental practices: the belief in power, and the belief in holiness or sacredness, i.e. in purification. These two great needs of early man were still strongly felt in early Greece, according to Martin Nilsson, the famous historian of Greek religion. We also find them in the early Hebrew religion as reflected in the Old Testament, and elsewhere. In fact, the Greek religion and the Hebrew are the two we know best, and they shed light upon each other at many interesting points, and at some which otherwise would be very obscure.

The oldest religions of the Ancient World were polytheistic, i.e. they were made up of the combined cultus of many different deities. Perhaps the most striking example is the religion of ancient Egypt, where there were not only the God of the North and the God of the South, combined in one as Amon-Rē, but innumerable lesser deities. Originally these were no doubt local gods; as Egypt grew into an empire, the local gods and their cults were gathered together, combined, rearranged, and reinterpreted, until the resulting pantheon finally emerged in the long central period in Egyptian history. The same was true of the ancient Sumerian, Babylonian, Assyrian, Aramaean, Hittite, and other religions in Western Asia: they were the result of the combined cultus of various cities, regions, and peoples. Here too was felt the need for power—i.e. for vitality, health, length of days; and for purification, i.e. for cleansing from ritual defilement or pollution, especially that which resulted from contact with blood, or the dead, or anything which was already "unclean". And here also there was a notable growth in the identification of law and justice with the will of the supreme god, and an attempt to stabilise society, or to retain conquests, by appeal to the sanctions of religion.

The religion of Ancient Greece was only partially expressed in the cultus of the "high" gods, the Homeric pantheon, Zeus and his heavenly court on Mount Olympus. In the dim background lurked darker deities, surviving from ages long before the invasion of Greece by the Achaeans, the Ionians, the Dorians, and other stocks which came in from the north. Down through the classical period, their cults were sometimes observed in secret; in the Hellenistic period (after 350 B.C.) they revived and their influences spread far and wide.

The old Roman religion was primarily an agricultural cultus, or group of cults, whose most marked characteristic was the painful, meticulous observance of ritual—so painstaking that if any error occurred in its recitation or performance, the whole rite had to be done over again. Under the influence of the Greek religion, which began to affect Roman religion at an early date but came in with a flood after the third century B.C., the Romans built temples, erected statues, collected oracles, and in general adapted their worship to that of the Hellenes— the "syncretistic" religion which, following Alexander's conquest of Egypt and the Near and Middle East, now dominated most of the Mediterranean world. Yet the burden of a cold, hard materialism, and the superstition which was never uprooted from paganism, the widespread astrology, and the growing belief in and practice of magic, eventually brought about the all but total collapse, not only of Roman religion but of Greek, and of all the ancient cults and beliefs which had come under their influence. Even the "barbarian" cults on the borders of the empire felt the change. A chill scepticism began to pervade the world's religious atmosphere.

Into this situation came two forces with a promise of fresh vitality: the worship of rulers, especially of the Roman emperors, and the so-called "mystery" religions. "The ancient gods are far away: thee we see face to face" —so began the hymn addressed by the Athenians to their "deliverer", Demetrius Poliorcetes, in 307 B.C. And in the cities of Asia (i.e. the Roman province in western Asia Minor) inscriptions were set up, hailing the Emperor Augustus, after his victory at Actium in 31 B.C. and his "restoration of the Republic", as the Saviour, Pacifier, and Protector of the whole world, the "God manifest" whose birthday was henceforth to be the New Year's Day for the whole province. But this worship of "divine men" failed, before long; for anyone could see that such rulers as Caligula, Nero, Domitian were not only not gods but in reality very wicked men, perhaps even insane.

The "mystery" religions came from the East: the cult of Magna Mater ("The Great Mother of the Gods") from Asia Minor, that of Isis from Egypt, Adonis from Syria, and so on. Only Mithras came from still farther east, from Persia. Essentially these were "primitive" (i.e. prehistoric) agricultural cults, designed to bring about the fertility of the earth and insure rich harvests for their worshippers. But under Greek influence, following the fourth century B.C., they were remodelled after the pattern of the ancient rites (the "mysteries") of Demeter at Eleusis. They now promised union with the god or goddess, and a blissful state in the world to come: the two ever-essential boons of purification (from sin and its pollution, both physical and moral) and power (i.e. renewed vitality and strength, both physical and spiritual). They did not promise immortality: that was already taken for granted by most men—by all but a few sceptical philosophers, though in time their influence spread widely over the Roman world, as many of the surviving epitaphs show. What the mysteries promised was a *blissful* immortality, a preferred status in the life to come, unavailable to those who had not received initiation in these ancient rites.

Some writers have maintained that the new Oriental mysteries influenced the young Christian religion, as it moved out from its birthplace in Palestine into the broad world of Graeco-Roman-Oriental civilisation, especially its conception of "a dying-rising god," the Saviour, and its twin rites of baptism and the holy supper. These two rites were more prominent in Mithraism than in any other "mystery", while the "dying-rising god" was found only in the originally agricultural cults, and not at all in the cult of Mithras. Moreover, the period when these cults

14

flourished most widely in the Roman world was the second to fourth centuries after Christ—and Christianity had been well started long before then. Finally, the specific character of the Christian religion was determined —so far as historical influences determined it—much more by its Jewish ancestry, environment, and antecedents (even including Baptism and the Supper, as we shall see) than by the far more distant and alien pagan cults.

Yet there can be no doubt of the eventual influence upon Christianity of the general religious outlook of men and women in the Graeco-Roman world, and especially their state of feeling, their attitude toward religion, and the hopes and aspirations they entertained. The Roman Empire, though a civilised and civilising power, was totalitarian, as far as religion was concerned. Any cult or religious movement which refused to recognise the state cult or the worship of Rome and the Emperor, or which seemed to threaten the stability of government, or to be a menace to public peace and order, was proscribed and prohibited, if necessary, persecuted and suppressed. One need not stress the immorality of first-century pagan life (as Christian apologists used to do); in fact, one cannot honestly contrast pagan society with that of our own days, in view of the vice and crime rampant in modern society. But in the first century there seemed to be no force available or adequate to counteract these conditions. Men were bowed down by astrological fatalism: everything had been determined in advance by the stars, and though magical rites might seem to set men free, at least temporarily or to a limited degree, the eventual triumph of a purely mechanical destiny was utterly inescapable. The mystery religions might solace the individual with hopes of a better state in the life to come—but they had nothing to say to society as a whole, or about any possible regeneration of the mass of men. The philosophers—many of them—taught a noble way of life, with the virtues of fortitude, temperance, justice, magnanimity; but they reached only a select few, chiefly in the upper classes of society. Slaves might be better treated, as time went by and as Stoic or Cynic teaching got written into law; but the accursed institution survived, and the owner of a slave—a fellow human being—was still permitted to torture him to death, under certain restricted conditions. It was a world ripe and waiting for the Gospel of Christ. The transformation would of course not come in a day or a year. In fact, it has not yet been fully achieved. But a beginning was made when Jesus began His preaching in Galilee: "The time is fulfilled, and the Kingdom of God is at hand; repent and believe in the gospel" (Mk. 1.15), and when the Apostles "went out and preached that men should repent" (Mk. vi.12). When the Gospel was proclaimed to the nations, it not only demanded *cleansing* from "every defilement of body and spirit" (ii Cor. vii.1) but also it promised "the *power* of an indestructible life" (Heb. vii.16). This is what all the world had been seeking, for countless generations. These were the two factors which had been most deeply involved in Greek religion, from the beginning.

Christianity and the World's Living Religions

As we have seen, the attitude of Christianity to the other living religions of mankind is not that all others are false, but that, as a rule, each contains some measure of truth, which Christianity contains in fuller measure; and that the limitations and defects in other religions, while shared by Christianity as a living religion, are shared to a lesser degree. Does this mean that Christianity is only *relatively* better than other faiths, and not absolutely or completely superior? Of course this is true: for the actual historical realisation of what Christianity essentially is, ought to be, and may in time become, is (as we have said) only partial and still far from complete. There are potentialities in the

Gospel which have never yet been realised. Hence instead of boasting about the superiority of our religion to all others, we simply invite men to study the Gospel of Jesus Christ, to come within the area of its radiant influence, to feel the power of its transforming message, to "taste and see", for themselves, "that the Lord is good" (Ps. xxxiv.8), to come and share with us in a priceless treasure, and to let God make over their lives, their homes, their society, their whole way of life under the guidance of His Holy Spirit. The real aim and purpose of modern Christian missions, both at home and everywhere else, is not competition but sharing.

One of the oldest religions in the world is *Hinduism*—a religion which in origin is older than the Vedas (the ancient sacred poetry of India), the Brahmanas (the priestly writings), and the Upanishads (the philosophical literature); and far older than the beautiful devotional poem, the Bhagavad-Gita. Technically, the historical sequence was Vedism—Brahmanism—Hinduism. The essence of this religion is belief in the transitoriness and even the meaninglessness of physical phenomena. The soul's experience in the midst of this dark vale of illusion is utterly deceptive. What one must do, therefore, is flee from the transitory to the eternal—a teaching not far removed from Paul's saying, "the things that are seen are transient, the things that are unseen are eternal" (ii Cor. iv.18). This escape from the evanescent and the unreal is possible, according to Hinduism, only after a long course of many successive lives—reincarnation is one of the cardinal principles of Hinduism—and at the end the soul will sink into the endless bliss of Nirvana. To most Westerners, Nirvana seems a state of pure negation, nothingness. To the Hindu, it means the loss of all that is temporal, phenomenal, accidental, imperfect, and union with the supreme and absolute Good which remains forever transcendent above time and place and all individual

17

peculiarities, even beyond every trace of individual personality. Popular Hinduism retains many of the features of ancient pagan cults, superstition, and even demonology. But its essential philosophy is closely akin to the "negative" mysticism found here and there in medieval Christianity, and elsewhere. With this the Gospel of Christ has little in common. For it takes for granted that men live only once, and then comes the Judgment (Heb. IX.27); that individual personality, being not evil but good, will survive (I Cor. XIII.12; I Jn. III.2); and that the world instead of being evil, a "vale of illusion", is really good (as its creator declared, Gen. 1.31) and awaits redemption rather than destruction.

Among other religions sprung from Hinduism, *Buddhism* is the most important. It is often described as "the religion of infinite compassion", and is based upon "the Four Noble Truths" which Gautama Buddha (*c.* 568-488 B.C.) taught in his attempt to free himself and others from the illusory present existence of mankind. These Four Noble Truths are: (1) All attachment to earth, or to life, or to love, is only suffering. (2) This suffering is caused by the thirst for existence, for growth, for power. (3) The total extirpation of this thirst, by the killing out of all desire, is freedom. (4) The way to the achievement of this goal is the "Noble Eightfold Path" of right belief, right decision, right word, right deed, right life, right effort, right thought, right renunciation. Since existence is suffering, the only way of escape is to renounce the desire to live. Moved by his deep compassion for suffering humanity, Gautama Buddha refused to enter Nirvana, at the end of his successful journey, and remained on earth to comfort and inspire, strengthen and uphold his followers. This motive reminds us of the great passage in Phil. II.5-11, where Paul described Christ as stripping Himself of all divine prerogatives, and becoming poor (cf. II Cor. VIII.9), a slave, and dying on the cross for the sake of mankind.

But instead of eventually entering Nirvana, Christ sits enthroned as Lord of heaven and earth—a very different conception from that of the perfect Buddha.

There are two main forms of Buddhism, *Hinayana*, or Southern Buddhism, the strict and original, self-abnegating and world-renouncing type, which has led to great asceticism in practice; and *Mahayana*, the Northern, which is gentler and more world-accepting. The former is found chiefly in Ceylon, Burma, Thailand, and Cambodia, the latter in Nepal, China, Korea, Tibet, and Japan, where the cultus of "Amida Buddha, our Refuge" is widespread. Those who have seen "The King and I", or have read *Anna and the King of Siam*, will recall the children's pantomime at the court school, and the references to "the kind Buddha" who rescued Eliza. Buddhism teaches purity, self-control, compassion, gentleness, loyalty —many virtues; it has much in common with Christianity, in spite of its world-renouncing outlook, and its almost total unconcern for social conditions in the present surrounding world. The saint closes his eyes to all these: are they not the result of accumulated penalties in lives misspent and not yet atoned or made good? To the Christian, poverty and disease are evils which must be done away and cease to blight the lives of helpless children, who are born into these evils by the process of generation, and not as a result of past guilt of their own or that of their parents (cf. Jn. IX.3).

In Japan, *Shinto*, "the way of the gods", is another "primitive" religion surviving, with modifications, into the modern world. In China, *Taoism* is likewise influential, while in India, once more, *Jainism* represents a reform of Hinduism somewhat parallel to, and also influenced by, Buddhism.

The basic religion of China is not Taoism but *Confucianism*, the admirable ethical system set forth in the Chinese Classics, the teaching of the political and social philosopher Confucius (551-478 B.C.), whose precepts sometimes parallel those of the Bible—e.g. on respect for parents. Childlike piety was the basis of all ethics, for this Oriental teacher. But the parallels do not go all the way, since the world outlook of Confucius was utilitarian, and his ethics only led to the greatest peace and advantage of the community in this life, as loyal subjects of a good and gracious king. The almost total absence of any thought of God seems to class it as an ethical philosophy rather than as a religion. For example, "If one sins against Heaven, to whom shall he pray?"

In Persia the teaching of the prophet Zoroaster (some time early in the first millennium B.C.) resulted in a reform of the old traditional agricultural and pastoral cults and the organisation of a new religion, variously known as *Mazdaism*, *Zoroastrianism*, or (in India) *Parsism*, which means only "religion of the Parsees," i.e. the Persians. It is a highly eschatological religion, emphasising the resurrection and the life to come, with a final Judgment of all men, all demons, and all angels. It is thoroughly dualistic, viewing the world as the battlefield of right *v.* wrong, light *v.* darkness, good *v.* evil, God *v.* Satan. It sets forth a noble standard of ethics, especially of truthtelling, for which the ancient Persians were well known among the Greeks and Romans. Many scholars think that the eschatological features in Mazdaism had an influence upon Judaism during the two centuries (538-331 B.C.) when Persia dominated all of Western Asia, Egypt, and even Thrace, with the result that eschatology (emphasis on "the last things"), the doctrine of the Last Judgment, the belief in resurrection and angels (Acts XXIII.8) came to receive far greater emphasis among the Jews. The Saviour of the Parsees is not Zoroaster, who was only the prophet of truth, but the Saoshyant who will come in the last age, conquer the remaining darkness, evil, and lies, and establish the true religion or the king-

20

dom of light. The seven spirits of the Apocalypse (cf. Rev. i.4, iv.5, v.6) have been thought to correspond to the *six* Amshaspands who surround the God of Light (Ahura-Mazda) and are named Good Thought, Right Order, Excellent Kingdom, Holy Character, Health, Immortality. But the correspondence sounds rather remote, and the heavenly figures are very much like the later gnostic hypostatisation of words.

Islam is the religion not only of the Arabs but also of vast and increasing numbers of people in Africa, Southern and South-eastern Asia, the islands of the Pacific, and elsewhere. It originated with Mohammed (A.D. 570-632) who reformed the inherited pagan religions and cults of the Arabs, under the influence, in part, of what he had learned of Judaism and Christianity, but, more largely, of his own intuitive understanding of religion and ethics, and the strange, overwhelming religious experience which he underwent when about forty years of age. His central conviction was: "There is no God but Allah, and Mohammed is his prophet." To this creed he added his proclamation, "in the name of Allah, the Merciful, the Compassionate," of the judgment to come, his call to repentance, and the threat of doom upon the impenitent. His moral and religious teaching was stern and severe, and included regular fasting, almsgiving (now a tithe), stated prayers, study, and—originally—participation in the "holy war" against unbelievers. Freemen were allowed four wives, the prophet more. Divorce was permitted, and remarriage with a divorced wife could take place only if in the meantime she had been the legitimate wife of another man. Wine, games of chance, and usury were all forbidden.

Muslims believe in the absolute sovereignty of Allah, the One and Only God, and in angels, Satan, Prophets, the inspiration of the Koran, the world to come, and predestination—these are the main dogmas. The *suras* (or

21

chapters) of the Koran are arranged, not chronologically but in order of length; but the order of development has been made out by modern scholars, both Muslim and Christian, and the psychology of the Prophet can now be more or less understood. Islam was—and is—a religion of conquest, and it came very near to conquering the whole Western world of the tenth to fifteenth centuries. In fact, Christians in north-western Europe were expecting its triumph, just before the tide turned with the discovery of America (in 1492), the relief of Vienna by Von Salm (in 1529), and the religious avalanche loosed by the Reformation (in 1516ff). There are many noble features in Islam, though a "social gospel" is lacking, and the few parallels with the Gospel of Jesus are more than offset by its militant antagonism to all unbelievers. Even so, it is possible to find some common ground with many individual Muslims, and to share with them in seeking the truths of religion as found both in the Koran and in the Christian Bible.

Many other cults and religions are "alive and on the march" in the modern world. But enough has been said, in describing briefly these outstanding classic faiths, to set forth the approach which many Christians now believe to be the correct one. There is no point in denouncing good, honest people who believe sincerely in the religion they have inherited from their fathers: such a policy is obviously futile, quite apart from the unfairness and injustice of it. Even the many cults here at home, which freely proliferate year by year, are not to be classed as false, evil, or wicked, but to be studied and understood. The doors should be opened wide for all men to see into the Gospel and find there the satisfaction of their spiritual and moral needs—whatever their religious allegiance. What matters is only that "Christ is preached" (cf. I Cor. xv.11).

22

I have said nothing about Judaism, but that is because the relations between Christianity and Judaism are different from, and far closer than, those between the Gospel of Christ and any other cult or religion. In a true sense, Judaism is the Mother faith of Christianity; in a true sense, Christianity is the "fulfilment" of Judaism— not empirical, actual, historical Christianity, which has failed often enough, but ideal Christianity, the religion of the Gospel, which simply takes Judaism for granted. A new day is dawning in the relations between Christians and Jews. And one of the most fruitful areas for exploration of common beliefs and hopes, religious ideals and aspirations, is surely that which is now often covered by the term, "the Judeo-Christian tradition". It is one of the features of the present book, I trust, that this area will become clearer and more important for those who study it carefully.

2

Belief in God

The Sources of Christian Belief

THE sources of the beliefs of the individual Christian are of course his home, parents, church, school, friends, community, books or journals he has read, and above all his own experience and reflexion upon it. From all these sources come ideas, impressions, convictions, hopes—or fears—which stay with him all his life, and mould his character. Hence the importance of proper religious teaching in childhood and youth: "As the twig is bent, the tree's inclined." Hence also the emphasis upon the "teaching office" of the Church, not only conspicuously in some churches but increasingly everywhere today—to make up for two or three generations of neglect. Many persons believe that the main source of Christian belief is the Church's teaching (or "doctrine," *doctrina*: teaching); but this is only one source among several. Aside from, or in addition to, the explicit teaching of the Church through its religious education programmes and otherwise, there is the constant impression made by sermons, prayers, hymns, conversations on religious subjects: all of these influence the growing Christian. Hence the acquirement of Christian beliefs is not wholly formal. "Informal tuition" is at least equally important. As Dean W. R. Inge of St Paul's in London used to insist, "Religion is caught, not taught." And yet, of course, the formal teaching of religion must never be neglected.

Perhaps we may add a few words, at this point, on some

of the terms used—and often misused—in referring to Christian teaching. *Doctrine*, as we have just seen, is what the Christian Church *teaches*. *Theology* is the technical study of this teaching by trained experts, who attempt to harmonise, unify, and articulate it as a system. Thus we speak of the theology of Wesley, of Hooker, of Luther or Calvin, of Thomas Aquinas or Augustine: each had his own system. As a rule, these theological systems were worked out and stated in terms of some philosophy or other: thus Augustine, in large measure, took for granted the Neoplatonism of his day; Aquinas, the Realist philosophy of the medieval schoolmen; Calvin, the modified scholasticism of his century—and so on.

Creeds and *Confessions* are the formal statements of Christian teaching which were drawn up by church councils for the purpose of refuting or rejecting views which were thought to be contrary to Christian teaching or which (as in the case of Gnosticism) threatened to undermine the whole Christian religion. *Dogmas* are the explicit, authoritative, formulated definitions of the Christian faith which the various churches require their members to accept. These are as a rule very few in number, though some persons complain of them as if they covered the whole body of Christian beliefs. For example, there is the "dogma" that Christ has "two natures, God and Man, in one Person"; or the "dogma" of the Blessed Trinity. But many of the most important Christian doctrines or beliefs have never been authoritatively defined, at least not by Protestants. The usefulness of creeds is obviously limited to the official repudiation of errors, i.e. of sectarian or heretical views which would undermine Christianity. They are not summaries of Christian doctrine as a whole, and many people question their use in public worship. Perhaps they would be more valuable if sung—for a hymn is not viewed as an infallible definition of religious truth. In fact the first use of a creed in public worship, at least in the West, is said to have been at Rome, at the midnight service on Christmas Eve about the year 900. Moreover, creeds might be better understood, as social or collective rather than individual affirmations of faith, if only the English translation were more accurate: the Nicene Creed begins, in Greek, not "I believe" but "*We* believe"—it is the church speaking and proclaiming its faith, not the private individual voicing his mature theological convictions after a long period of thought and research! It is probably our "Western" type of mind, overawed by scientific pursuits and achievements, especially since the seventeenth century, which is responsible for the equating of theology, dogma, or creeds with religious beliefs or convictions. We almost instinctively demand concreteness, accuracy, explicitness of definition, and demonstrable, factual statement, even when dealing with religious truth or the foundations of man's inner life. But our religious views and attitudes, our deepest beliefs and convictions cannot be stated that easily! A poem, a prayer, a hymn, a painting, a noble human character tells us far more about religion than any "scientific" theological formula can possibly convey. There is of course a proper place for creeds and confessions of faith, for dogmas and theology; but it is a real question whether these are the best means to use in the teaching of religion, as encouraging a child's growth in Christian faith and practice, in Christian morals and belief, in the Christian "way of life".

For the true sources of Christian belief are much deeper than creeds or formal definitions. They are nothing less than the whole Christian tradition, from the first century to the present, and back of that the whole Hebrew-Jewish tradition, reflected in the Old Testament and in the religious convictions taken over by the early Christians from ancient Judaism and from early Christian Judaism in Palestine. This is a living religious tradition,

26

voiced in many ways, in hymns, prayers, sacred books, stories, works of art—and not only in the formal theological statements which were issued from time to time. In a word, the ultimate source of Christian belief is *the Bible*, i.e. the divine revelation contained, recorded, or reflected in its pages. There was a time when it was said that "the Bible, and the Bible only, is *the religion of Protestants*" (this was almost the exact title of William Chillingworth's famous book in 1637). But those were days of fierce controversy, both within the Protestant world and outside it. And the words could easily be—and were—misunderstood, as if they meant that anyone by reading the Bible for himself could write his own creed, devise his own theological system, organise his own church, even ordain himself a minister. But the major Protestant churches never went as far as that: The place of *the Church*, as the teacher of Christian faith and morals, as the home of the Christian soul, as the place of divine worship, must not be ignored by anyone concerned with Christian teaching. For it is the Church which handed the Bible down to us. First of all it collected and safeguarded the sacred books in days of persecution, and then preserved, copied, and recopied them; and it has translated, retranslated, and expounded them, through the long centuries since those early days, in every quarter of the globe. It is the Church which is still the teacher of the Christian faith, and she continues to teach with the Bible open before her.

Hence it is not the "literal" Bible, torn from the Church's hands, or lifted out of the living tradition of life and worship inculcated by the Church, which is our source of doctrine. It is the Bible as read, studied, expounded within the Church, which is our major source of belief. We must try to avoid a dull, wooden literalism which would ascribe inspiration and infallible authority to every word, every punctuation point.[1] Instead, we

[1] Even the traditional translations, e.g. the Authorised Version, or

27

should listen for *the Word within the words, the Gospel within the gospels*, the living message from God to men which is still being transmitted to us through this ancient collection of sacred writings. The true meaning of the slogan, "the Bible, and the Bible only, the religion of Protestants," is that no institution, no man, no church official, no group of officials, no formal theological pronouncements—and certainly no secular officials or pronouncements—can be received, or permitted to stand, in lieu of the Word of God speaking through the words of inspired seers and prophets, Apostles, or the divine Son of God. The "open Bible" was on the side of religious liberty. This is where it has always been, ever since the sixteenth century, when modern Biblical scholarship began. It was then that the historical, literary, philological study of Holy Scripture took the place of the fantastic allegorical, purely theological or ecclesiastical interpretation which for centuries had made it say whatever was uppermost in the interpreter's mind.

God the Creator

The very opening words of the Bible affirm that "in the beginning God created the heaven and the earth" (Gen. 1.1). The whole central point of Biblical religion and of Christian belief is involved here: when God began to create, "the earth was without form and void, and darkness was upon the face of the deep"—the primeval chaos, conceived as a vast ocean—"and the Spirit of God—or a great wind—moved over the face of the waters. Then God said, 'Let there be light.' And there was light . . ." (Gen. 1.3). The ancient Greek literary critic known to us as "Longinus" said that this was the most sublime passage

---

Luther's German Bible, have been so treated; there were, of course, no punctuation points in ancient Hebrew or Greek manuscripts—though punctuation is often more important than the words, in determining the meaning of a text!

28

he had ever read. Its sublimity is not lessened for us by
our modern views of the universe, or for example by radio-
astronomy which can even pick up the sounds of collision
between whole galaxies, 270,000,000 light years distant,
where creation is still in process—or where, as someone
has suggested, the Day of Judgment has begun. For
despite the discoveries of modern physics and astronomy,
the existence of the universe is no better explained today
than it was in the Book of Genesis. Why should it ever
have come into existence? What is its real meaning and
purpose? When did it begin? When and how will it
end?—or will it ever end? And what are we?—only
insignificant denizens of a tiny speck of matter in one of
the obscurer parts of the universe, flitting swiftly about a
slowly fading sun which is considerably off-centre, even in
our own super-galaxy, in what is after all only a relatively
dim and quiet corner of creation? So modern science
would seem to suggest! But the ancient Biblical writer
faced a similarly unconcerned universe: Marduk and the
other gods, some said, had slain the primeval monster,
Tiamat, and out of her carcass, split and gutted like a fish,
had formed the heaven above and the earth beneath—a
myth much like the Egyptian, where the back of the
cosmic cow formed the Milky Way. As over against this
popular mythological idea—which really explained nothing—the Hebrew poet affirmed that "in the beginning
God *created* heaven and earth". It was His doing, and His
purpose controlled everything. The destiny of the universe
was in His hands, and the destinies of all men and all
nations. As one of the psalmists set forth the same idea:

By the word of the LORD the heavens were made,
[i.e. by His creative utterance, not a mere exhalation],
    and all their host by the breath of his mouth (Ps. xxxiii.6).

Thus God created the universe, and thus He created man
—the psalmist who composed the glorious hymn of

creation, Psalm VIII, had a similar idea. The weakness and insignificance of man, his glory and his possibilities are God's handiwork, for he is made in God's image (see also Psalm XIX).

In Buddhism, as is well known, there is no god, but only the rigid, inescapable *Karma* or law of existence, by which "whatever a man sows, that he will also reap" (Gal. VI.7), and which tracks him down through innumerable successive lives until his sins are expiated and his empirical self is cast aside like an old garment, and he enters at last into eternal oblivion. In the Bible, man is amenable to God, but it is to God his Creator, who made him, who loves him, who longs for him, and who in the end redeems him from eternal death, extinction, and nothingness.

In Islam, on the other hand, God is the Creator and Judge, but the Merciful One is also very stern, so that men can only tremble before Him, and bow to meet their inevitable fate, their doom or destiny. But stern as is the God of the Old Testament, His sternness is that of a Father, and even His most rigorous enactments are laws "by whose observance man shall live" (Ezek. XX.11 and 13)—as a human father forbids his child to play with fire.

> The Lord is loving unto every man:
> And his mercy is over all his works.
> (Ps. CXLV.9, B.C.P.)

In the Greek religion, beautiful as it was in many ways, the gods themselves were helpless within the universe—not its creators—and *Moira*, blind destiny, stood behind each of them as it stood behind every mortal. No god could deliver a favourite from death: at best he could only prolong his days a little (cf. Ps. XXXIX.15, B.C.P.), but in the end he could do nothing more for him. And men were continually shortening their own appointed span of life, and increasing their allotment of woe, by their incorrigible, unaccountable folly—this is the repeated lesson in classical religion, from Homer down. "See how ready mortal men are to blame the gods! For they say evil comes from us, whereas through the blindness of their hearts they bring upon themselves sorrows beyond what is ordained" (*Odyssey* I.32-34). "They would not hold back their hands from evil, and so through their own blind folly they met a dismal doom" (*Odyssey* XXII.317).

But over against all this, the sublime affirmation of the Hebrew writers that God is the Creator of the universe, that God is man's Maker and Judge, stands out like a shaft of clear sunlight as it shines through a lowering sky, dark and overcast with clouds. Again and again this truth is affirmed, from beginning to end of the Bible. God is "the Creator of the ends of the earth" (Is. XL.28). It is He who "teaches men knowledge" (Ps. XCIV.10). It is He who calls up the generations of men, and shows His loving-kindness to thousands (Ex. XX.6). "His judgments are in all the earth" (I Chron. XVI.14); yet "mercy and truth are met together" (Ps. LXXXV.10, A.V.). The great affirmation with which the *Shema* begins—i.e. the three passages of scripture (Deut. VI.4-9, XI.13-21; Num. XV.37-41) learned by heart and recited twice a day by every Jew—proclaims this central truth in unforgettable words: "Hear, O Israel, the Lord our God, the Lord is One!" And it continues: "And you shall love the Lord your God with all your heart, and with all your soul, and with all your strength" (cf. Mk. XII.28-30)—to which Jesus added as the "second commandment" the words of Lev. XIX.18, "You shall love your neighbour as yourself" (Mk. XII.31).

The same conviction is affirmed in the early Christian baptismal creed (the so-called "Apostles' Creed"): "I believe in God the Father Almighty, Maker of heaven and earth." Here the words were chosen in order to rule out the teaching of the early second-century Gnostics, who held that instead of an act of creation, the universe

31

was the result of a system of graded emanations, from the Supreme or Absolute Being down to the level of formless matter; and the Greek word for "Almighty" was really *Pantokratōr*, the All-ruler, the One who makes all things obey him, who brings good out of evil, who compels even "the wrath of man to serve him", who overrules the devices and purposes of men, and guides all the processes of history. That magnificent conception, set at the very forefront of the Church's earliest creed, came from nowhere in the pagan world, but only from the Old Testament, from the sacred Scripture of the Jews which was now also that of the Christians. We easily take for granted, today, this unique idea of the sovereignty of God the Creator—and we even stumble over its plain-speaking. But there was really nothing in the world like it, in the first or second century, except in the Jewish-Christian Bible. That is where the central affirmation of our belief came from.

A famous English scholar, H. Wheeler Robinson, has written a book on *Inspiration and Revelation in the Old Testament*, (Oxford 1946,) a volume that every Christian teacher and student should study carefully. In it he sums up the revelation of God as described in the sacred Hebrew Scriptures. It is taken for granted that God reveals Himself—for man does not by searching, or by speculation, or by accident, come upon Him (cf. Job XI.1-7, XXXVIII.1-XLII.6). He reveals Himself in three ways: (1) through nature, as the Creator and Sustainer of all things; (2) through history, especially in the events of Israel's call and commission, the events of the Exodus and the settlement in Canaan, together with all the ups and downs of political and religious history thereafter; and (3) through human life, especially human character, the lives of saints and heroes, of godly men and women who hearken to His voice, obey His will, and find peace and happiness in their fellowship with Him. Among these are the prophets, the "speakers for God" who declare His will and deliver His commands. To the righteous, the devout, to those whose one aim in life is to do "the will of their Father in heaven", He opens pathways of joy and refreshment which are otherwise unknown:

> The path of the righteous is as the dawning light,
>   That shineth more and more unto the perfect day.
> (Prov. IV.18; A.R.V.)

And in the end,

> The souls of the righteous are in the hand of God,
>   and no torment will ever touch them.
> In the eyes of the foolish they seemed to have died,
>   and their departure was thought to be an affliction,
> and their going from us to be their destruction;
>   but they are at peace.   (Wis. III.1-3)

The Doctrine of the Trinity

It is a popular modern view that the Christian doctrine of the Trinity is the product of speculation by ancient Christian philosophers or theologians. They took their cue from paganism, it is said, and created a purely theological or "metaphysical" idea of God, which they substituted for the living God of the Bible. The Greek and Roman cults worshipped triads: Jupiter, Juno, Minerva; Osiris, Isis, Harpocrates; and so on. And the Christian formula, "Father, Son, and Holy Spirit," was only one more of these triadic conceptions of deity; the difference between Christianity and paganism lay only in the Christians' insistence upon the divine unity. On the other hand it has been held, by theologians, that Trinitarian belief is superior to Unitarian because it allows for a "social" existence within the Godhead, the divine "society" of the Three Persons in one God. This argument for Trinitarianism has often been advanced by orthodox theologians.

But the history of early Christian doctrine does not bear out either theory. Both theories assume that the Church began with three gods and later found it necessary to combine them into one. Instead, Christianity began as a religious movement within Judaism, which (as we have seen) was a strictly monotheistic faith. One might say that instead of moving from polytheism—which was pagan—toward monotheism (or Unitarianism), the Church began with a unitarian, purely monotheistic conception of God and moved forward to a view which deserves some better name than "Trinitarian"—let us call it *Triunitarian*. For the Church still insisted firmly upon the unity of God, though recognising His Tri-unity. It was a unity of three "persons", or "hypostases", or "centres of consciousness" —all these are crude ways of attempting to say what it is really impossible to say, to define, or even to conceive. In fact, "unity" or even "trinity in unity", is meaningless unless it implies a unity, i.e. a union, of things or persons conceived as somehow separate or distinct. How this union is possible, we do not know. In theology it is called a "mystery."

Now the way all this came about seems clear from the New Testament and the other early Christian writings. To begin with, no early Christian thought of God in any other way than as the one Person described in the Old Testament and in Jewish teaching and worship: the Creator, the King, the Father of His people, the Father of the individual who worshipped, loved, and obeyed Him. The only *new* element in the Christian belief in God, which distinguished it from Jewish belief, was the emphasis upon God's freshly revealed purpose to bring the present evil age to a speedy end, to hold at once the Last Judgment upon men and nations, and to establish His universal divine Kingdom without further delay. His Messiah had already appeared—He had come in order to proclaim the Kingdom of God, to teach, to heal, to call and prepare

34

men for the impending divine Reign; He had died as a sacrifice or expiation for human sin; He had risen again, victorious over death; and He would come soon, in glory, to hold the Last Judgment and to reign as God's Vice-gerent over the renewed world. This did not mean that Jesus was "God"—no Christian Jew could have said that, nor would the later Church say it; the strictly orthodox definition was always "God and Man" or "the God-man". But it certainly came as near to calling Him "God" as a basically monotheistic or unitarian religion could come. The simple formulae found in the New Testament (e.g. II Cor. XII.14, Mt. XXVIII.19) presuppose that Jesus, now exalted to heaven, and standing—or seated—at God's right hand, is not only in the presence of God but shares the divine existence. The very title "Lord" (Phil. II.9-11) carried connotations of divinity, i.e. of deity, for everyone in the first century who knew and understood Greek. It was the title the later emperors used when they claimed divinity (as Domitian did, calling himself *dominus ac deus*: "lord and god"). It was the word used in the Greek translation of the Old Testament, the Septuagint, for the Hebrew name of God. ("Yahweh" becomes "Lord", *kyrios*, in the Greek translation.) Hence the problem for Bible-reading early Christians in the Gentile, Greek-speaking world. Christ somehow represented God; He "manifested" or "revealed" or "declared" Him—as in Jn. 1.18, XIV.8-11, XVII.4-26. Or He existed originally in the "form" (*morphē*) of God (Phil. II.6), i.e. "he lived a divine existence", as Martin Dibelius translated the line. Or He was the divine *Logos* or "Word", with God from before the creation of the world, the one through whom or by whom God created all things, who finally took our "flesh" (i.e. human nature) and lived here upon earth—as in Jn. 1.1-14; cf. Heb. 1.1-4. Or He was "one with God the Father" in an even profounder sense: the "Modalists" of the second century believed that God was revealed

35

"successively" as Father, Son, and Spirit, i.e. the Son *was* God the Father, and hence when the Son suffered on the cross it was the Father who suffered. Hence they were called "patripassionists", as holding that God the Father had suffered. But none of these was a final or even a satisfactory solution of the problem. The whole long story of early Christian theology, from the first century to the fifth, and even later, centres in the attempt to find a satisfactory brief *statement*—not necessarily a satisfactory definition or explanation—of the relation between Christ and God as it is reflected in various parts of the New Testament.

A similar problem ran concurrently with this one: How was the relation of the Spirit to the Father and the Son to be conceived or stated? In the Old Testament, the Spirit of God was "poured out" upon prophets and seers, and they prophesied, or saw visions. In the famous prophecy in Joel III.1-5 this was predicted, in fullest measure, of the coming Golden Age when even the slaves in Hebrew households would be inspired to supernatural utterance. From the very beginning of Christian history, as it is recorded in the New Testament, the "outpouring" of the Holy Spirit is taken for granted (Lk. III.22, IV.1, 14, 16-21; Acts 1.8, II.1-4). In a true sense early Christianity was a "pneumatic" or "spiritual" movement. The strange and unusual phenomena of speaking with tongues (I Cor. XII-XIV), of performing miracles, especially of healing the sick and exorcising demons, were ascribed to the Spirit which lived in the Church and acted through its members. It was Paul who insisted that the "fruits of the Spirit" were not extraordinary, bizarre, wonder-working powers, but the ethical-religious qualities observable in a consecrated life: "love, joy, peace, patience, kindness, goodness, faithfulness, gentleness, self-control" (Gal. v.22). The divine gift was usually received at baptism (Acts XIX.1-7), but it might even precede the

down into the material world of darkness and matter, where the body of flesh and human nature lay "entombed" in the dreadful realm of the physical senses and appetites. But the Church rejected this neat and picturesque system with its "dualistic" presuppositions—i.e. of a world of evil opposed to the world of good; of malevolent spiritual powers arrayed against God and almost as powerful as He; destined to be conquered in the end, but meanwhile all but destroying the world which God had made and which He had approved as "good" (Gen. 1.31). If we had lived in the second or third century, we would probably— let us hope—have agreed with the majority of Christians in rejecting all such systems of speculation, and clung to the simple language of the Bible, the Creed, and the Liturgy—regardless of whether or not we could explain, or even understand, the divine relations (divine "economy" was the word then used).

All this needs to be said today, for a great many modern Christians are deeply troubled by the doctrine of the Trinity, and both those who reject it and—sometimes— those who defend it agree in viewing it as something far more speculative and philosophical than it really is. Of course there were, later on, profound interpretations of its inner meaning, or value, or necessity, or truth. But historically viewed, up to the fifth century, the doctrine of the Trinity was chiefly an attempt (a) to play fair with the language of the New Testament and maintain "the proportion of the faith"; (b) to rule out one-sided interpretations and misinterpretations which would have turned Christianity into either one more Graeco-Oriental mythology or a fictitious, syncretistic metaphysical system which substituted words for entities; and (c) to safeguard the right of the historical faith to live and breathe freely in a world where theosophical speculation threatened to close in upon both philosophy and religion.

As Bishop Charles Gore used the illustration, in his

famous Bampton Lectures on the Incarnation, the Christian creeds were like the village green in old English towns: this was a space which must be kept open at all costs, and neither baron nor squire nor yeoman was allowed to encroach upon it, to alienate it, or encumber it with buildings. Here the poor man must be permitted to graze his cow or sheep, here the labourer must be allowed to rest beneath its spreading shade. The creeds were not designed to confine the truth, but to *prevent* its confinement by any alien system of thought or terminology. If the effort had not been made, or if it had failed, the Christian Church might possibly have become as extinct as Mithraism or the cult of Isis, and an all-dominant dualistic philosophy (e.g. Gnosticism) might have crushed and smothered the spirits of men.

But it is a pity the Church did not stop at this point, and refuse to encourage further speculation in a realm where the human mind, by its very nature, is incapable of forming clear-cut concepts and of turning the mystery into a mathematical demonstration. For example, the so-called "Athanasian" Creed undertook to elaborate a definition which should be binding upon all Christians: "Whosoever would be saved must first of all hold the Catholic faith. . . . Now the Catholic faith is this: We worship . . . the Trinity in Unity." Of course this creed was not written by Athanasius, but was a later composition, possibly in the fifth century, designed to anathematise the Priscillianists, a heretical sect then flourishing in Spain and Southern France—some scholars say the Apollinarians, a century earlier. But for many centuries this creed was viewed as the official statement of the doctrine of the Trinity in the Western church, and was still in use in some churches until quite recently. It is a question if the deepest impression left by this far too dogmatic statement was not, after all, the existence of three divine beings who were somehow, inexplicably, one and the same. This certainly is not the doctrine of the New Testament, which —as we have seen—starts with the *unity* of God, and never yields that central principle. The Father, the Eternal Creator and Ruler of the universe, is revealed by the Son and by the Spirit; the Son, "the man Christ Jesus," the historical Jesus of Nazareth, is the Teacher and Saviour, the exalted Lord of the Church, the Son of God who became man, who died, who rose again, and now sits at God's right hand; the Spirit is the experienced Power of God, the revealer of God, the inspirer of the prophets and of the holy writings, "the Lord and the Life-Giver" who "proceeds" from the Father and the Son (or *through* the Son: East and West are divided on this point) and who brings life and light to the world. The process of thought, in the New Testament and in early Christianity, was not from Trinitarianism to Unitarianism—from three gods to one—but from the divine unity to the divine tri-unity, still strongly maintaining the divine unity in spite of all tendencies toward tritheism or a kind of triadic personality. The long quarrel between Trinitarians and Unitarians should never have taken place—at least not on the grounds commonly alleged. Each group misconceived or misinterpreted the position of the other—and sometimes its own.

3

Sin and Forgiveness

Man's Relation to God

FROM the outset, as we have seen, the Bible views God as a person, not as a force (*numen*) or finite spirit (*daemon*), a principle, or a universal law; this is what chiefly distinguishes the Bible from many other religions. As a person, God is approachable, can be addressed, listens, hears, and answers the appeals of men. He is "the God who speaks" and whose "mighty acts" have been designed to help and guide His people. In fact, as the Bible insists from its very beginning (Gen. 1.26f), God created man "in his own image and likeness", i.e. with a rational, spiritual nature like His own, and unlike "the beasts that perish" who are mere "flesh" (cf. Is. xxxi.3). Therefore all idolatry, both the making and the worship of material representations of God or of a god, is utterly wrong. The prophets and the later Biblical writers never ceased to castigate, ridicule, and satirise the worship of idols, which was then common throughout the rest of the world. The Jewish Temple in Jerusalem was famous for its lack of any statue or other "likeness" of God—a fact which in A.D. 40 led the mad emperor Gaius ("Caligula") to attempt to set up his own statue there.

Hence the religion of the Bible is a "rational" religion, from the outset, not a mass of primitive superstitions held together by loyalty to a local or national deity, from which men could be only slowly and painfully set free by prophets and reformers. True, there was superstition enough in the ancient Semitic world, as elsewhere in the Greek, Roman, Hindu, and Egyptian areas. But Hebraism began with the work of a prophet, Moses, who apparently proclaimed the sovereignty of the one God, Yahweh, who had chosen Israel to be His own people, manifested Himself to them, declared to them His will, and undertook to use them as His chosen instrument for His self-revelation to mankind and in His guidance of the course of history. To this proposal—or "call"—the nation's fathers at Mount Sinai had responded, "All that the Lord has spoken we will do" (Ex. xix.8; note the repetition in 1 Esd. ix.10). Henceforth Israel was closely related to God as His own special (or "peculiar," i.e. his very own) people, a fact which laid upon them special duties, i.e. the observance of the sacred Law in all its details. Modern Biblical research has shown how this view gradually arose in Israel in the course of several centuries, and how the Law, instead of being delivered *in toto* at Mount Sinai or on the plains of Moab, gradually grew, as one level of legislation was accumulated above another. But the general or resulting conception of Israel's covenant with God was the one described above. There were other gods of other peoples—so at least it was generally assumed; but the Israelite could proudly ask, "Where is there a god like our God?"—"a God merciful and gracious, slow to anger, and abounding in steadfast love and faithfulness, keeping steadfast love for thousands, forgiving iniquity and transgression and sin, but who will by no means clear the guilty, visiting the iniquity of the fathers upon the children and the children's children to the third and the fourth generation" (Ex. xxxiv.6f). And though the Semitic peoples as a rule assumed that their codes of law were inspired and ordained by their own gods (Marduk, for example), the simple truth is that the Old Testament code contained far more humane provisions than most others did, laid stronger emphasis upon

43

genuinely ethical requirements (as contrasted with cere-
monial), and pointed the way more clearly toward further
advances in religion and morals. The "ethical monotheism" which resulted was no accidental development,
but was implicit in the Hebrew religious outlook from
the beginning. As the horizon widened, the prophets
insisted that God's concern for men included other nations
as well as Israel. In the end, in spite of their long oppres-
sion of the Hebrews and the fierce hatred that had grown
up between them, "Israel will be the third with Egypt and
Assyria, a blessing in the midst of the earth, whom the
Lord of hosts has blessed, saying, 'Blessed be Egypt my
people, and Assyria the work of my hands, and Israel my
heritage'" (Is. xix.24f). Israel's mission was peace: this
included the political unification, the moral and social
regeneration, the deepened spiritual insight of all mankind, when "the earth shall be full of the knowledge of
the Lord as the waters cover the sea" (Is. xi.9), when all
nations shall come to Jerusalem to learn the true religion;

> For out of Zion shall go forth the law,
> And the word of the Lord from Jerusalem.
>
> (Mic. iv.2)

Where else, in the whole Ancient World and among its
many cults and religions, was there any similar ideal of the
unity of mankind, or of world peace under the one God
and Father of all? The answer clearly is: Nowhere else.

Even when the actual course of history betrayed and
contradicted such optimism, and the nation went down
to defeat before Assyria (Samaria, the capital of the
Northern Kingdom, fell in 721 B.C.) and Babylonia
(Jerusalem, capital of the Southern Kingdom, fell in
597-586 B.C.), the great "prophet of the Exile" commonly
called "the Second Isaiah" came forward to explain the
meaning of this tragedy. Israel and Judah had been
punished for their sins—they "had received double" what

they deserved, at God's hands, and would now be "comforted" (Is. xl.1). But their sufferings had been vicarious: the penalty for the sins of the other nations as well as for their own had been laid upon them. The suffering "Servant of the Lord" (i.e. the Jewish people, according to most modern scholars) was the sacrifice which God Himself had provided for human sin, to be offered before the new and final age of righteousness and peace could be inaugurated.

> Surely he has borne our griefs
> and carried our sorrows;
> yet we esteemed him stricken,
> smitten by God, and afflicted.
> But he was wounded for our transgressions,
> he was bruised for our iniquities;
> upon him was the chastisement that made us whole,
> and with his stripes we are healed. . . .
> . . . the Lord has laid on him
> the iniquity of us all. (Is. liii.4-6)

Where else, in the whole Ancient World and among its many cults and religions, or among all the prophets, wise men, or philosophers of history, was there any similar interpretation of national tragedy and disaster, redemption and restoration? The answer again is: Nowhere else. Whether or not one believes the interpretation to be inspired, it is certainly sublime, and unique. We Christians believe that it is all this and more, for we cannot fail to view it as an anticipation or prophecy of a still deeper fulfilment when Christ died on the Cross "in accordance with the scriptures" (1 Cor. xv.3).

The Problem of Sin

The Bible is a very ancient book. Its oldest parts take for granted many of the ideas common in South-western Asia during the centuries which saw Israel's settlement in Canaan and its growth into a nation. The traditions underlying its earliest books or their component sources are older still—some of them certainly as old as Hammurabi and the brief Semitic rule which he established in Mesopotamia, in "the land of the two rivers", about 1700 B.C. Some of these ideas are so different from ours today that considerable thought and imagination are required if we are to comprehend them. Fortunately, we now have a vast accumulation of literature—or even whole surviving literatures—from other ancient peoples, shedding light upon early Hebrew ideas and customs. Among these, no books are more important that those of the Greek poets and historians, especially Homer, Hesiod, the tragedians, and Herodotus. For they still retain, refer to, or explain many of the "primitive" (i.e. prehistoric) religious ideas and practices which were later abandoned or rejected, as civilisation advanced; and it is these which also underlie some of the older parts of the Hebrew Bible.

Not only is this true—and valuable for our understanding of the Scriptures—but it is true also that these books and traditions help us to understand human nature, human conduct, and human character as it exists today— and always. "Mankind is always advancing; man remains ever the same," said Goethe. And the facts about human nature laid bare by modern psychiatry or psychoanalysis bear out this saying. Socrates and the Stoics were wrong: man is *not* essentially a rational being, who needs only to see what is right to do it, or to be convinced of a truth to put it in practice. Underneath the surface lie dark cavernous depths in the human *psychē*, which is either an "unconscious" or a "subconscious" mind, or an inherited mass of subhuman, perhaps even animal patterns of instinctive behaviour, or a nature which lies between the "mind" and the "flesh" (to use New Testament language) and embraces both. The human mind is like an iceberg—not in temperature or rigidity, but in the fact that seven-eighths of it lies beneath the surface.

These "deeps below deeps" are no figment of the imagination, but very real—as the modern practice of psychotherapy demonstrates. And it is no wonder that modern psychoanalysis has turned to the Greek myths (reflected chiefly in the tragedies) for some of its most important terminology—e.g. the figures of Oedipus, Orestes, Andromache, Electra, Medea, Ion, Hippolytus.

Not only psychotherapy, but also the scientific study of criminal behaviour makes use of these facts. For it is now discovered that deep within the *socio*-pathic individual, as within the psychopathic, lie hidden levels of semiconsciousness, or of unconsciousness, which must be reached, healed, and transformed if he is to become a responsible member of society. The experts find at least three of these deeper levels: (*a*) at the dark abysmal bottom level is a realm of *fear*, whose driving terrors sometimes explode into mad, uncontrollable violence (we have always known that most hatred springs from fear; for men do not love or honour but hate what they deeply fear); (*b*) somewhat higher is a level on which the individual feels a sense of *pollution*, ostracism, alienation, infection, incurable corruption, so that he is loathsome even to himself (if he possesses enough moral insight or "conscience" to be aware of what he has done or become—even a faint glimmering of conscience or of conscientiousness is enough); (*c*) still nearer the surface is a level on which a sense of *guilt* is found, which presupposes a much more fully developed moral sensitivity, a feeling of personal relation and responsibility, the result of indoctrination by a code with a consequent awareness of social standards. It is no use trying to "reach" a mind on level (*a*) with appeals proper to level (*c*): the result is a merely formal, purely superficial acknowledgment of guilt; driven by insane terror or hatreds born of fear, the "guilty" person will repeat his crime all over again—even after punishment he is basically the same person he was before.

It is obvious that all this means a complete revolution and transformation, not only in modern medicine but also in modern penology. The distinction is also recognised by anthropologists, who now distinguish between a "shame culture" (the heroic, more or less amoral age or level) and a "guilt culture" (where personal relations have been moralised, and where breaches of the moral law involve something more than mere disgrace). But what concerns us here is its bearing upon the interpretation of the Bible, and upon our own beliefs (or "theology") as based on the Bible. It also affects pastoral work, religious teaching and counselling or spiritual direction, and social service.

The very terms we use, which are borrowed from the Bible, and were age-old when the Bible was written, must be kept distinct and not confused. Such words as "Atonement"—i.e. the process of becoming, or of being made, "one" with another person once more, a process which requires something to be given or done in order to heal the breach between them; or "Reconciliation"—the result achieved by this restoration of normal good relations; or "Expiation"—the performance of whatever is necessary in order to re-establish the broken order, restore the "peace of the gods" (*pax deorum*), or the invisible, supernatural system of relations between men and the Unseen World; or "Redemption"—the "buying back" of a person alienated from his God or his social group, by payment of a "price" (cf. Lev. v.18, xxv.47-49); or "Sacrifice"—which is sometimes offered to God or the gods, but may (as in Gen. xxii.8, 13) be provided by God for the purpose; or "Propitiation"—which implies the anger of God (or the gods), who must be placated or appeased before the divine wrath destroys the group—all these terms are deeply embedded in ancient religion, and are retained and used in Christian worship, teaching, and theology with some of their original meaning left out, and

48

the remainder modified or transformed. But it only leads to confusion to view them as interchangeable, or to use them without noting their distinct meanings. To describe the death of Christ as a "propitiation" clearly implies an angry God who must be placated by the death of a sinless person; but this is not the meaning of the New Testament—and the Revised Standard Version rightly translates *hilasmos* by "expiation" (see 1 Jn. 11.2, 1v.10).

Further, to stress the sense of guilt as the sole requirement for repentance or conversion is to mistake the seriousness of the situation, in many a human life. What is needed is the love that "casts out fear," not a mere word of pardon. What is driving a person deeper into sin and alienation from God may not be guilt at all, or even fear, but a sense of pollution—of an infection or corruption which is eating his heart away, and which neither forgiveness nor reassurance—that his guilt is forgiven and done away or his fears groundless—can do anything to help. What he needs is to be cleansed, made pure once more, and given the power *not* to sin again, i.e. a spiritual prophylactic against reinfection. These are not mere metaphors, all describing one and the same thing, but are attempts to describe three very different states of mind, pollution, guilt, and fear. To treat as a sense of guilt what is really a sense of pollution, or a shattering fear, is like treating measles when the case is really typhoid fever, or bronchitis when the patient is dying of tuberculosis. Much popular religious diagnosis, one suspects, is tragically superficial. A confession of guilt is often easy to obtain—it is like a polite "I'm sorry". But to acknowledge in oneself the deeper states of alienation is harder; often the sinner is not himself aware of their existence, so completely do we deceive ourselves and pretend there is "nothing the matter".

One of the most important facts brought to light by modern research in the history of religions, chiefly of

Greek religion, is the sharp distinction between sin as pollution and sin as guilt. Of these two conceptions—or feelings—the former is clearly the more deeply laid, i.e. the earlier, the more ancient and "primitive". We find it clearly presupposed in Greek literature. In Sophocles' great play, *Oedipus the King*, the whole land suffers from the pollution (*miasma*) spread over it by an ancient crime, whose entail is producing still more wickedness and suffering, as generation succeeds generation, until in the end the accumulated poison wrecks the health, the peace, and the happiness of the whole Theban city-state, and destroys the innocent King Oedipus himself. In the Old Testament similar ideas are found. For example,

> He [God] turns rivers into a desert,
> > springs of water into thirsty ground,
> a fruitful land into a salty waste,
> > because of the wickedness of its inhabitants.
>
> > > > (Ps. cvii.33f)

One thinks also of such passages as the Song of Moses (Deut. xxxii), and the terrible story of famine due to a curse, and its expiation (ii Sam. xxi).

This level of thought about sin, as something physically corrupting and infectious, only slowly gives way to the purely personal conception which we find in the Psalter and the later parts of the Bible. Both conceptions are embedded in the penitential psalm:

> Have mercy on me, O God,
> > according to thy steadfast love;
> according to thy abundant mercy
> > blot out my transgressions.
> Wash me thoroughly from my iniquity,
> > and cleanse me from my sin!   (Ps. li.1-2)

So far (vss. 1-2), the older, "primitive" conception provides the pattern of thought and language: what "pollution" requires is cleansing—as nowadays "atomic fallout" or radioactive pollution can be removed only by vigorous scrubbing. But at once the psalmist sweeps to a higher level of personal faith, devotion, contrition:

> For *I know* my transgressions,
> [Oedipus and others did *not* know]
> > and my sin is ever before me.
> > *Against thee, thee only, have I sinned*
> > and done that which is evil *in thy sight.*
> > > (Ps. LI.3-4)

The rest of the hymn acknowledges this guilt, and God's righteous judgment upon it, and pleads for forgiveness as well as cleansing and the creation of a new heart and mind, the implanted gift of God's own holy Spirit, and the sinner's restoration to divine favour—something which animal sacrifice cannot effect (vs. 16) but only "a broken and a contrite heart" followed by God's gracious forgiveness and renewal. (Vss. 18f are obviously a later addition to the psalm, quite out of tune with the rest.)

Is Sacrifice Necessary?

Jewish scholars question the Christian interpretation of Christ's death as a sacrifice for sin, and the assumption that divine forgiveness was impossible apart from the vicarious sufferings of Jesus on the cross. God's forgiveness is free and unlimited; it is conditioned solely upon the sinner's genuine repentance. This view, we must admit, is found everywhere in the teaching of Jesus, for example in the Parable of the Prodigal Son: "He arose and came to his father. But while he was yet at a distance, his father saw him and had compassion, and ran and embraced him and kissed him" (Lk. xv.20). Nowhere does Jesus suggest or even imply that divine forgiveness is conditional on His own death. In fact it would not be full and free forgiveness, if God required some *quid pro quo* (which a pagan god was thought to demand of his worshippers) before He would grant forgiveness. The whole idea that forgiveness must be purchased is pagan, not Biblical, and it was terribly exaggerated and even caricatured by the theology and devotion of the Dark and Middle Ages, when God was often pictured as weighing each ounce of Christ's suffering and granting an equivalent amount of forgiveness in return. Here was another example of a theology which did violence to the conception of God, and it should have been repudiated once and for all (see Chapter 1). But it still lingers on. A great evangelist in our time has proclaimed, "God demands blood. Without blood there can be no forgiveness." And many devout Christians are convinced that this is so; they therefore try their best to "accept" the impossible doctrine, despite the protest of their own conscience and their deepest religious convictions. Others frankly reject it, but feel that in so doing they have cut themselves off from orthodox Christianity, and certainly from the teaching of the Bible. But this is not so. If only the Reformation had gone further in its promotion of Biblical research, if only it had not lapsed back into a kind of "Protestant Scholasticism" or "Biblicism" in the seventeenth century, with results that survive to this day, we should long ago have seen more deeply into the real meaning of the Scriptures.

The trouble arises, very largely, from failure to distinguish the terms we use. Even Paul used these terms obscurely, as in Rom. v; though it is clear from Rom. vi and from the whole argument in Rom. v-viii that his solution of the problem is mystical, not "forensic" or legal. *Forgiveness* of sin applied only to guilt, or indebtedness. (Jesus usually looks upon sin as a failure to do what one should: hence "forgive us our *debts*," in the Lord's Prayer.) *Cleansing* from sin or *removal* of sin goes deeper. It applies to pollution, infection, corruption—the older and more "primitive" idea of sin, especially in view of its social consequences. The earliest conception of sin, like the earliest ethics, was social or communal, applying to a whole group of people, not individual or personal. When the early Christians described the death of Christ as "for sin" or "for our sins" they meant, not that He died in order to win God's forgiveness, but for the *removal* of sins— both the actual sinning and the consequent contamination. For example, when John the Baptist testifies, "Behold the Lamb of God, who takes away the sin of the world!" (Jn. 1.29; and this is certainly the testimony of the author of the fourth gospel) this probably refers to the death of Christ, but only in a general way; what is important is the actual *removal* of sins, their destruction or annihilation, the cleansing from both personal and age-old social sins which have polluted men and still alienate them from God. The Epistle to Hebrews is full of the same idea: not guilt, but pollution, corruption, disease and death must be taken away, as once the scapegoat was thought to remove the sins of the people and "bear" (i.e. carry) them away into the wilderness (Heb. vii.26-x.22). Sins have been "purified" by Christ (Heb. 1.3—i.e. *men* have been purified from sin). This is something far deeper, psychologically and historically, than the idea of forgiveness—which, as Jeremiah and others had seen long before, rendered all sacrifice meaningless and unnecessary. "Behold, the days are coming, says the Lord, when I will make a new covenant with the house of Israel and the house of Judah, not like the covenant which I made with their fathers . . . my covenant which they broke. . . . I will put my law within them, and I will write it upon their hearts; and I will be their God, and they shall be my people. And no longer shall each man teach his neighbour and each his brother, saying, 'Know the Lord,' for they shall all know me, from the least of them to the greatest, says the Lord; for I will forgive their iniquity, and I will remember their sin no more" (Jer. xxxi.31-34). This is not one more national covenant, to be inaugurated with sacrifices and maintained by a cultus with a hierarchy of ministers; it is

53

designed to *take the place* of all such primitive worships, at once their fulfilment and their abrogation (as the Epistle to Hebrews correctly interprets it). It is the fulfilment of the Psalmist's prayer:

> Create in me a clean heart, O God,
>   and put a new and right spirit within me.
>   (Ps. LI.10)

When this is done, there is no more need for sacrifice—for sin itself is done away, brought to an end: men simply will not sin any more!

Fundamentally, as we now recognise, sacrifice and cleansing were originally one and the same, and were devised with the same object in view. This identity is written all over the records of ancient Greek religion. In *Odyssey* XXII.482ff, Odysseus bids Eurycleia bring sulphur and cleanse the house of its pollution, "and bring fire, and purge it"—the thing which sacrifices, incantations, offerings, magic herbs and "cuttings", rites of expiation and cleansing were expected to effect (see Aeschylus, *Suppliants*, 260-270). In *Iliad* 1.313-316, the son of Atreus orders the army to purify itself, cast the defilement into the sea, and offer Apollo appropriate hecatombs of bulls and goats on the shore. It is the actual *removal* of pollution, not a mere "pronouncing clean" that is required—as in the Christian liturgies the Lamb of God "takes away" the sin of the world: *O Agnus Dei, qui tollis peccata mundi!* In the "primitive" cults of Greece and Anatolia, the *pharmakos* ("medicine"), whether an animal or, at times, a man, was first led about the city, in order to absorb and gather into itself (or himself) the impurity which caused the pollution, contagion, or contamination; it (or he) was then made away with, driven over the borders, killed, or burned. The ancient Hebrew rites of the Day of Atonement, with its "scapegoat" (see Lev. XVI), are closely parallel.

Fundamentally, our Jewish critics are right. God does not "demand blood" before He "can forgive". Such "forgiveness" would be an immoral farce. God's forgiveness is free, full, and unhesitating, dependent only upon the sinner's complete repentance and his free, full, unreserved acknowledgment of his sin. He must also, Jesus added, forgive all who were likewise indebted to him, as he was indebted to God: the "sins of omission" are as serious as those of "commission." The prayer which He taught the disciples included the petition,

> Forgive us our debts,
> as we also have forgiven our debtors;

and to it He added, "For if you forgive men their trespasses, your heavenly Father also will forgive you; but if you do not forgive men their trespasses, neither will your Father forgive your trespasses" (Mt. vi.14f). The penitent must also make restitution, and as fully as possible undo the wrong he has committed—as in the story of Zacchaeus (Lk. xix.8f). As the Baptist had taught, he must begin the practice of charity, justice, and good will (Lk. iii.10-14). Finally, he must "go, and never sin again"—Jesus's parting word to forgiven sinners (see Jn. v.14, viii.11).

The New Life in Christ

As to *why* we sin, Christianity has no answer, for it is no system of speculation, theological or anthropological, but simply recognises a fact, namely that all men *do* sin, and "fall short of the glory of God" (Rom. iii.9-18). The later theory of the "Fall of Man", as the old tale in Gen. iii was interpreted, is not explicitly stated in Scripture— but only in ii Esd. (=iv Ezra) vii.116-126, where we hear the tragic cry, "O Adam, what have you done? For though it was you who sinned, the fall was not yours alone, but ours also who are your descendants" (vs. 118). *O tu quid fecisti Adam!* rings across the ages like a cry of despair, one of the most tragic lines ever penned. It is echoed in *The New England Primer* (1690),

> In Adam's fall
> We sinnèd all,

and also over wide areas of Christian thought, devotion, theology, poetry, and art. The nearest the New Testament comes to this idea is in Rom. v.12, " . . . sin came into the world through one man and death through sin, and so death spread to all men *because all men sinned*"; and in Rom. VIII.22, "the whole creation has been groaning in travail together until now"; but the doctrine of the Fall of Man is nowhere clearly set forth in the Bible. It is a later inference or interpretation.

What the New Testament really emphasises is the new life which is ours in Christ: "If anyone is in Christ, he is a new creation" (II Cor. v.17). Christ is "the beginning of God's [new] creation" (cf. Rev. III.14). Old things have passed away: "Behold, I make all things new" (Rev. XXI.5). We are buried with Christ by baptism into His death and likewise raised in His resurrection (Rom. VI.3-4), an idea which carries at its heart the idea of a mystical union, or even an identification, of the believer with Christ, so that he suffers with Christ, dies with Him, is raised with Him, is glorified with Him, and now sits with Him "in the heavenly places" (Eph.1.20,II.6). This is *a new religion*, relatively to the religion of the Old Testament and Judaism, and even as compared with the teaching of Jesus according to the Synoptic Gospels; it is found in St John's Gospel, chiefly in ch. xv. But its antecedents are to be found in the older religion. For the Bible as a whole assumes that God's purpose all along has been redemption. God made man to be immortal (Wis. II.23; cf. II Esd. VIII.59); but, through sin, death entered the world, and hence God could save men only by a special act which would set them free from death. This act of God was viewed at first only as the prolonging of men's days upon earth (Deut. IV.40), then later as a climactic event to take place "in the latter days" when the dead would be raised and the righteous enter into bliss (Dan. XII.2; see also the other apocalyptic writings). In other words, the Bible knows nothing of any "natural immortality" to which all men are entitled—the conception of Sheōl, in the Old Testament, like the Greek idea of Hades as set forth in Homer and in other writers, is of a wholly undesirable kind of "eternal habitation" (Ps. CXV.17; cf. *Odyssey* XI. 488-491, "Nay, do not speak comfortingly to me of death, O great Odysseus! I would rather work in the fields as a poor hireling, even for some poverty-stricken man with a scant livelihood, than reign over all the dead.") "Eternal life," on the other hand, is something new, and is conferred—or conveyed—through the knowledge of Christ and fellowship with Him, through baptism, through martyrdom, through partaking of Christ "the living Bread," through having His spirit within one: these are all different descriptions of the same experience, the same hope. The idea that man was meant "not to die" (as in the Book of Wisdom), but forfeited his immortality by sin and disobedience, represents a combination of the Greek idea of the natural immortality of the soul with the traditional view of human sinfulness and unworthiness of the divine gift. It is Christ who confers eternal life—or who restores it; He also restores man's forfeited freedom of will, which has been lost through his enslavement to sin (Rom. VII).

Similarly, there is no idea, in the Bible, of a natural and inevitable progress of society upward and onward toward perfection. That is an idea peculiar to the nineteenth century and the early years of the twentieth (prior to 1914), though traces of it have been detected here and there in earlier periods, and even in ancient

Greek writers. It presupposes the theory of evolution, of which the Bible knows nothing (evolution may of course be a true theory, and it probably must be accepted; but it certainly is not found in the Scriptures). Instead, the Bible views the world as created a relatively short time ago (Archbishop Ussher's date, 4004 B.C., is only one among many calculations based on the Biblical data). It also assumes that the end of the world is rapidly approaching. Even in the Old Testament the prophets refer to "the latter days", which are soon to be upon them. In the New Testament it is expected, in the gospels, that "this generation will not pass away till all these things take place" (Mt. XXIV.34), though the evangelists allow for a period, of undefined length, during which the Gospel must first be preached "to all nations" (Mk. XIII.10). Paul expected the end of the age momentarily (as in I Thess. IV.13-17), and assumed that he and his readers would face it. In the Apocalypse of John, written c. A.D. 95, the author believes that Jesus is returning soon: "He who testifies to these things says, 'Surely I am coming soon.' Amen. Come, Lord Jesus!" (Rev. XXII.20). And the prayer of the early Christians was, "*Marana tha*": "Our Lord, come!" (I Cor. XVI.22), echoed in the Didache (x.6), "Let Grace come [or 'let Christ come,' as some scholars conjecture]; let this world pass away."

Throughout the New Testament and in many other early Christian writings, the whole sky is red with the beams of the approaching new day. There are two things to be noted about this: (1) *Eschatology*—the belief in a final goal to all God's purposes from the creation of the world—is as fully taken for granted in the Old Testament as in the New. A world which has disobeyed God, continually contravenes His purposes, and thwarts His will, cannot possibly endure. God will not be frustrated or defeated. And so through all the ups and downs of history—the rise and fall of empires, the wickedness of kings or their righteousness, the sending of prophets, judges, deliverers, and their acceptance or rejection—God is always at work (Jn. v.17). God is "working His purpose out." As Lord of history, and equally as Lord of Creation, His wisdom and His will must triumph in the end:

> The Lord sitteth above the water-flood:
> and the Lord remaineth a King for ever.
> (Ps. xxix.9, b.c.p.)

The classical Greek and Roman, especially the Hellenistic, view of the universe as endlessly repetitive, going around forever in cycles, coming back every 10,000 years, or every 26,000, to the same position and then repeating the whole round once again—that view was impossible for the Hebrew, the Jew, the early Christian. The pagan could hold it, because for him the gods were really inside the universe, and as completely subject to Moira (Fate or Destiny) as any other creatures or phenomena of nature. But the Jew and the Christian could not think in these terms, because for them God is transcendent, outside the universe, above it, the Creator of all things, the One who called them into existence and commanded them to obey His will. Such a symbol as that of the Hellenistic *Aiōn* (Endless Time), viz. the hoop snake with its tail in its mouth, "chasing itself," rolling on forever in endless cycles of existence—such a symbol was not only meaningless but even abhorrent to the Christian. To him it only symbolised a prison, like a squirrel cage in ceaseless, futile rotation. To him, the arrow launched on its course, the ship setting sail on its journey, or the Cross as "the sign of spreading forth in heaven"—these were more fitting symbols of his faith.

(2) The New Testament also takes it for granted that this final realisation of all God's purposes, from the creation of the world, is not only about to take place but *has already begun*. This is the meaning of what is often called

"realised eschatology". It does not mean that God's Kingdom is wholly here, or completely realised, but that its realisation is already under way. "But if it is by the Spirit of God that I cast out demons, then the Kingdom of God *has come upon you*" (Mt. xii.28). That is how Jesus Himself viewed and interpreted His own exorcisms, cures, and "mighty works". The writer of the Epistle to Hebrews describes Christians as "those who have once been enlightened, who have tasted the heavenly gift, and have become partakers of the Holy Spirit, and have tasted the goodness of the word of God *and the powers of the age to come*" (Heb. vi.4f). The "mighty works" of God through Christ, of Christ through the Apostles, of the Holy Spirit through the Church—all these are the beginning of the New Age, and proofs of its advance. "Two worlds are ours"—not the inner and the outer, but the present and the future; and the two overlap. The old order is becoming obsolete, and is about to vanish away (cf. Heb. viii.13); the new is arriving, and will soon be fully realised "with power" (Mk. ix.1; cf. Lk. x.18f.) The spirit of the whole New Testament is reflected in Sir Owen Seaman's poem, written during World War I:

> I saw the powers of darkness put to flight,
> I saw the morning break.

It was not just the forgiveness of past sin, or even the removal of present sin—the penitent being left with the unhappy expectation of sinning again—that the early Christians desired and to which they looked forward. Instead, it was to be the end of all sinning, the power *not* to sin, in a world where "sin shall be no more", and where, with sin abolished and done away, death would also naturally cease—"the last enemy to be destroyed is death" (1 Cor. xv.26). The old dragon, Satan, the Tempter, "the accuser of our brethren", Apollyon the Destroyer, would be bound for a thousand years in the bottomless pit and eventually destroyed, and then would come the New Age, the new world "wherein dwelleth righteousness". And to this day that is still the heart of the Christian hope.

4

Belief in Christ

The Christian Creed

THE Christian believes *in* God. This is something far
more than believing that God exists, and that He is
the kind of Person described in the Bible and in
Christian teaching. It means personal trust, self-com-
mittal, and deep confidence in the One who is our Father
in heaven. "Whom have I in heaven but thee? And
there is nothing upon earth that I desire besides thee"
(Ps. LXXIII.25). As Martin Luther translated it, "If I have
but thee, I will not ask for things in heaven and earth."
The Christian also believes *in* Jesus Christ (Jn. XIV.1)—
as the Apostles' Creed states it, "*in* Jesus Christ his only
Son our Lord". And then the Creed goes on to describe
Him as the one "who was conceived by the Holy Ghost
[i.e. the Holy Spirit], born of the Virgin Mary, suffered
under Pontius Pilate, was crucified, died [not 'was dead'],
and was buried; he descended into hell [*Hades*, the place of
departed spirits]; the third day he rose from the dead;
He ascended into heaven, and sitteth at the right hand of
God; from thence he shall come to judge the quick [i.e.
the living] and the dead." As a description—it is not a
definition—of Jesus Christ, this leaves many modern
Christians puzzled. Why is there no mention of His
teaching, His character, His influence, His Apostles, His
Church, His inspiring example, or His atoning death?
A generation ago, in the heyday of "Modernism", efforts
were made to enlarge this creed and introduce clauses

which would mean more to present day believers. Some went so far as to draw up "modern" creeds, "social" creeds, affirmations of present-day Christian theology or doctrine. But these have all disappeared. As Edwyn Bevan said, in his excellent little book, *Christianity*, the advantage of the ancient creeds is that they *require* interpretation: no one thinks of taking them literally (e.g. "he descended *into hell*", "he ascended *into heaven*"), as one must take a modern creed.

It will be worth while to pause for a moment and consider what the ancient creed meant, and why it was composed. The oldest form of our Apostles' Creed, which is the basis of most later creeds (e.g. the Nicene), comes from the second century. It was in early use as the Christian profession of faith at baptism, following the renunciation of "the world, the flesh, and the devil". And it was one of the three strong bulwarks thrown up against Gnosticism, a system of theosophy which threatened the very existence of the Christian faith. Gnosticism began, apparently, in the first century. Simon Magus (Acts VIII.9-24) is said to have been its founder. Certainly it was flourishing early in the century following. Its fundamental tenet was the identification of evil with matter. Pure spirit, the divine nature, divine grace, God's revelation must be removed as far as possible from contact with the evil material world, the flesh, and everything physical. Hence the supreme deity, who is wholly beyond the world and therefore totally unknown—the "Wholly Other", as some modern thinkers describe Him, the "Unknown God", or the "Invisible King"—cannot possibly come in contact with this present evil world, even to create it. Another god, a subject deity, must have been its Creator or *Demiurge*; and this other god was identified with the God of the Jews, who was not only the Creator of the world but also the giver of the Jewish Law (which most Gnostics rejected). Between the Supreme

Being, throned in light, and the darkness here below, there is a whole ladder of supernatural beings, essences, powers—such as Wisdom (*Sophia*), Truth (*Alētheia*), Silence (*Sigē*), and so on. These fill the space between God and man—for man lies helpless at the bottom of the scale, drugged and inert in a miry dungeon beneath the lowest sub-cellar of the universe. Since matter is evil, and since physical life is dependent upon it, marriage and the bearing of children are wrong: the true Gnostic (i.e. the one who "knows") must therefore abstain from marriage. Further, since a divine being cannot come in contact with matter, and certainly cannot die, Christ's physical body must have been unreal, a mere phantom or "appearance", and before the first nail was driven at the Crucifixion His spirit must have fled to the supernal realm of purity and light—the Roman soldiers only nailed a corpse to the cross. This whole fantastic theory was designed, no doubt, to show greater reverence for Christ, but it only made Him completely unreal, a mythological figure, an apparition flitting lightly above the dark soil of earth and never in real contact with it. If this theory had prevailed, the whole of the historical element in Christianity would have been softened and absorbed, as by a chemistry that destroys the bones.

Against this perversion of Christian teaching, the Church appealed to three authorities which would make clear and unmistakable the view which had always hitherto been held: (1) *the apostolic writings* (approximately our New Testament, which includes no "gnostic" books); (2) *the apostolic tradition* (the succession of the Church's teachers, the bishops in the chief centres or "sees"—e.g. Jerusalem, Antioch, Ephesus, Rome); and (3) *the apostolic creed*, which summarised the teaching of the Apostles on these contested points. The creed was not a summary of all Christian belief: our "Modernists", a generation ago, did not recognise this—and some writers still do not, even today. Its only purpose was to rule out the gnostic mis-interpretation of the Christian faith. God is the Al-mighty, the All-ruler, the *Pantokratōr* (see p. 32); there is no graded sequence of "aeons" between Him and the material world. It is He who is "the Maker of heaven and earth." Christ is His *only* Son; there are no astral "elemental spirits of the universe" (Col. ii.20; cf. Gal. iv.9) sharing His sovereignty and thereby limiting it or re-belling against it. He is our *Lord*: the only Lord (Phil. ii.11; Rev. xix.16)—the phrase goes back to one of the oldest liturgical or confessional statements in the New Testament (i Cor. xii.3, "Jesus is Lord"), which in turn rests back upon the Aramaic ejaculatory prayer: "*Marana* (Our Lord) *tha* (come)!" (i Cor. xvi.22). Jesus had been viewed as "Lord" almost from the beginning of the Christian faith. He was "conceived by the Holy Spirit, born of the Virgin Mary"—the point is not to affirm the Virgin Birth, which is simply taken for granted on the basis of Mt. 1.18-25 and Lk. 1.34f, but to emphasise the reality of His human nature, His physical body. If certain other texts had been chosen, e.g. "the son of Joseph", as in Jn. vi.42, or "the son of Mary", as in Mk. vi.3, the purpose would still have been the same, namely to stress the physical reality of His birth. This we see also in Jn. 1.14, which goes the length of saying, not that He "took our nature upon him"—as the Church later affirmed—but that He "*became* flesh". This shows how serious was the crisis presented by the Gnostics: St John's Gospel is the chief *anti*-gnostic writing in the New Testament. As St Irenaeus said, the Gospel of John was written to counteract Gnosticism, especially that of Cerinthus (*Against Heresies*, iii.11.1).

Moreover, the creed omits all mention of Jesus' ministry and proceeds to describe His suffering, His death, His burial, His resurrection. Why? Clearly it was in order to continue the emphasis upon the physical reality of His body, which Gnosticism denied. The final phrases of the creed still emphasise the "corporeality" of the Christian hope: the old Latin creed, which was probably the original form of the Apostles' Creed, does not say "the resurrection of the body," in agreement with 1 Cor. xv and with practically all Christian theology since, but "the resurrection of the flesh" (*resurrectio carnis*), as if to drive home its anti-spiritualist conviction, and show that Gnosticism was utterly untenable in its view of God, Christ, and the Christian's one hope of life to come. The same is true of many other brief statements (not "summaries") of Christian faith in this embattled area, not only in the New Testament but also just over the horizon in the early second-century letters of Ignatius of Antioch, and the somewhat later writings of Irenaeus, Hippolytus, Tertullian, and others. For the struggle against Gnosticism—and the kindred systems of thought which arose later—lasted for a long time. Marcionism and Manichaeism were still in existence in the Middle Ages. Moreover, their influence has survived in various areas of Christian thought, and still distorts Christian teaching as it is understood or viewed by many people at the present day.

Christology

What is meant by the "divinity" of Jesus Christ? As the Church affirmed it, almost from the beginning, our Lord's divinity meant that He was God's representative, agent, or revealer, who came into the world to teach the truth about Him, to act for Him, to die as a sacrifice for sin, and to rise again and return to God as His glorified Son. One of the most important "Christological" passages in the New Testament is Phil. ii.5-11. Here the doctrinal statement really comes in as an illustration: Paul's point is the selfless devotion expected of the Christian, and he shows how it was exemplified by Our Lord. Some

66

scholars think that the passage was a hymn, possibly composed by Paul himself, and now quoted by him as a reminder to his readers of the teaching about Christ which he had already given them. Christ had been originally "in the form of God", or, to adopt the translation by Martin Dibelius, "He lived a divine existence". He was either one of the sons of God who lived in the heavenly courts (as in Job 1.6), or He was the unique and "only" Son (John 1.18). But as contrasted with Satan, who yielded to the Titanic temptation (according to an age-old myth in the Near East and in Greece) and undertook to storm the heights of heaven, dethrone God, and seize control of the universe, and also as contrasted with Adam, who was made in the divine image and then longed to be "like God" (Gen. III.5), Christ did not look upon "equality with God" as something to be seized (*harpagmon*: "seized," not "grasped" or "clutched"). Instead, He "emptied himself," i.e. He utterly denied and abased Himself, stripping off His divine prerogatives, powers, and title, and "took the form of a slave", being "born in the likeness of men . . . in human form". And so He "humbled himself and became obedient unto death" (i.e. even to the extent of dying, as a man), "even death on a cross"—the most shameful, and perhaps the most painful, of all possible forms of death. "*Therefore* God has highly exalted him," and has granted Him the name or title which is "above every name," namely the title *Lord*, at the mention of which every knee must bow, "in heaven and earth and under the earth"—for angels, demons, men, and spirits of the dead must all worship Him. (Cf. Heb. 1.3b-13.)

It is this pattern of thought which underlies all of Paul's thinking about Christ, and also much of the thought about Him in the rest of the New Testament. For example, in 1 Cor. xv.23-28 Paul describes the continuing further process of the establishment of God's

Kingdom, in stage after stage: Christ's rising from the dead, i.e. His victory over death, is the beginning of a period of conquest during which this victory is carried further. Every "rule, authority, and power" which oppose God must be destroyed; Christ "must reign until he has put all his enemies under his feet: the last enemy to be destroyed is death"—for death is the consequence, as Paul believed, of sin, whether human, angelic, or demonic. Then at last Christ will return victorious from the war; He will gather His own followers about Him (1 Cor. xv.23), and hand over the conquered, unified, and restored Kingdom to God the Father (1 Cor. xv.24).

This was Paul's "plan of the ages", the mysterious programme that God had kept secretly in mind from generations and aeons long before (Col. 1.26), but which now His Son was carrying into effect. It was this great conviction of the triumph of Christ at His resurrection, and of His future even greater triumph at the end of the present age, which supported Paul and the early Christians in their darkest hours. What mattered persecution, opposition, suffering, even martyrdom, in view of the invincible progress of Christ's conquest of the surrounding alien world of demons and spirits, and of men—including wicked rulers—who were in the power of these demonic forces? The "divinity" of Christ, for the early Christians, was not a neat theological formula, but a battle cry—as in the Book of Revelation, where Christ goes forth "conquering and to conquer" (Rev. vi.2), with His thigh symbolically emblazoned "King of kings and Lord of lords" (Rev. xix.16). We simply cannot understand the New Testament Christology unless we transport ourselves, by sympathy and in imagination, to the little Christian churches scattered over the Roman Empire, their very existence threatened by a totalitarian political power and by malicious enemies—anti-Christian Jews and pagans—who would wipe them from the earth, if they could.

A time came when the Church was at peace (relatively!) under the "Christian" emperors, and when theologians undertook to harmonise and correlate the data of the New Testament, the creeds, and the Church Fathers. It was believed that Christ was of "two natures [God and Man] in one person", and so the problem arose of explaining how this was possible. But again—as we have seen in Chapter 2—the Church did not try to explain, or even to define, but only to stake out the area within which these affirmations could be made. And in order to stay within the normal limits of Christian faith and worship, it was necessary to say (a) that both of Christ's two natures were real: He was "truly" (alēthōs) God and at the same time "perfectly" (teleiōs) man; and also (b) that His two natures were combined, not identified; they were united "inseparably" (achōristōs) and yet "inconfusedly" (asungchutōs), "without change" (atreptōs) and "without division" (adiairetōs); one nature did not become the other, as some fourth- and fifth-century teachers held. Of course this is not the language of the New Testament but of a later age, like that describing Christ as "of one substance with the Father" (homoöusios) and not merely "of a similar substance" (homoiousios). Edward Gibbon, in his famous Decline and Fall of the Roman Empire, ridiculed these hairsplitting distinctions, and so likewise have many other people. But, without granting the propriety—or the possibility—of making such metaphysical statements, it is clear that the Church faced the necessity of ruling out the strange, bizarre, unhistorical views which were then being promulgated and popularised, as two centuries earlier the views of the Gnostics had been popularised. The Church was compelled to act, and it made use of strange new terms in order to refute strange new views. On the whole, the Church's point of view was faithful to the New Testament and the historical tradition of the Christian faith.

For in the New Testament Jesus is certainly the "Prophet" of God (Lk. IV.24, VII.16, XIII.33; Acts III.22-26; Jn. VI.14, VII.40), the "Revealer" of the Father (Mt. XI.25-30), the "Witness" (Jn. III.31-35) or "Messenger" whom God has "raised up and sent" to His people Israel. This conception of Christ's office or nature, probably the earliest of which we have any trace, underlies the whole development of New Testament Christology. The old variant forms, such as "a man who went about doing good" (Acts II.22, x.38) or God's "servant" (Acts III.26, IV.27, 30), the "Leader and Saviour" (Acts v.31) or "the holy one [i.e. the saint, *chasid*] of God" (Mk. 1.24; Acts III.14), were scarcely Christological "titles" at all, but only popular descriptions. This is what people called Him in Galilee and Judea during His lifetime. Even "the prophet Jesus from Nazareth of Galilee" (Mt. XXI.11) is not a Christological title, but only a popular descriptive term. So also may have been the designation of Him as "Son of David" (Mk. x.47; cf. XI.10); the early Church did for a time hold that this term really described Him, as the genealogy in Mt. 1.1-17, the tradition in Rom. 1.3, and other passages clearly imply. Jesus Himself seems to have questioned, perhaps even to have repudiated it (Mk. XII.35-37). It was the slogan of the nationalists, and had been so for a long time (see Ps. LXXII):

> Behold, O Lord, and raise up for them their king, a son of David,
> At the time which thou choosest, O God,
> That he may reign over thy servant Israel.
> (Psalms of Solomon XVII.21)

But Jesus had no intention of heading a revolution, driving out the Romans, and mounting a throne in Jerusalem.

Later titles and conceptions included that of "Lord", which probably meant at first the head of a cult, one who was worshipped by his followers, not as God but as a divine being, subordinate to God, the invisible head of a religious community: this was a widespread conception throughout the world of the first century. The use of the term *Mar* ("Lord"), in the phrase we have already quoted from 1 Cor. xvi.22, which goes back to the old Aramaic-speaking Christian community in Palestine, certainly pointed in the direction of the later Church's worship and theology. In fact, the Church was already moving steadily in that direction. When the Church spread out into the vast Greek-speaking world of the "Gentiles," where the Jews were already using a Greek translation of the Old Testament (the Septuagint) and in consequence were calling God by the title *Kyrios* ("Lord"), it was only a step for the Christians to identify their own *Kyrios Christos*, "the Lord Christ", with the God revealed in the ancient sacred writings of the Hebrews. The importance of this identification for the later development of Christ-ology is clearly to be seen in the New Testament (e.g. Mk. xii.36; Lk. xx.42; Acts ii.34; 1 Cor. 1.31; Rom. x.13) and is written all over the early "patristic" literature, i.e. the writings of the early Church Fathers.

Still other terms and titles are well known, from the New Testament and all of Christian literature since the first century. Thus Christ is our "Redeemer"—Paul uses this figure to describe how Christ "bought us from slavery and set us free"—though it is only a figure of speech for a spiritual fact really passing description or explanation. He is also our "Saviour"; this was a divine title (*Sōtēr*), long used in the Greek world, not only for one who had rescued another person, or his city or country, but for one who preserved it, and maintained its safety or welfare. He is likewise the "Son of God", which is not a Jewish Messianic title (as one rabbi said, "God *has* no Son") but was the dearest title for a divine being known to the Hellenistic world. It connoted a supernatural person who had voluntarily remained on earth and devoted himself to human welfare: a "Son of God" like Asclepius the Healer, or Heracles the Deliverer. Christ is even the "Logos", the "Word" of God by which, or through which, or by means of which, God had created the world (Jn. 1.1-14), now "hypostatised" and viewed as a divine being who was in the presence of God, "with" Him, before the creation of the world, and His agent in the act of creation (cf. Prov. VIII.22-31).

These terms and titles the early Gentile Church took over and transformed, making them adequate for Christian use, and thus emphasising the promise of divine help and succour which had been implicit in the titles from the beginning. For now at last "the goodness and loving kindness of God our Saviour", His gentleness and His love for man (*philanthropia*, Titus III.4), for which the pagan world had been longing, was fully manifest in Christ. This longing was likewise a "testimony" to Jesus, equally as valid as the prophecies found in the ancient Hebrew Scriptures.

For it is obvious that these were all attempts to set forth the meaning which Christ had now come to possess for Christians—what Henry Sloane Coffin called "the portraits of Christ in the New Testament". They were not formal theological definitions, and in time many of them were abandoned. No one, as Rendel Harris once remarked, would ever think of singing, "How sweet the name of Logos sounds"! Even the barbers of Alexandria, who set Arianism to music and sang popular songs as propaganda, would never have thought up such a line!

However, two titles are found in the gospels, which, as many modern scholars believe, go back to Jesus Himself, viz. "Messiah", and "Son of Man". (*a*) The one, Messiah, denotes the "Anointed" King of Israel in the glorious Age to Come, a figure not really divine but divinely endowed, with supernatural powers and prerogatives. All ancient Oriental kings were thought to be thus equipped, as adopted "sons of God" (see Ps. ii.7-9) and His representatives on earth. The question whether or not Jesus used this title of Himself—or accepted it when used of Him by others—can be answered only by surveying the whole gospel tradition. It is impossible to settle it by appeal to the High Priest's question in Mk. xiv.61, or to Jesus' affirmative answer, which "bends the barb" and looks in another direction: "I am; and you will see the Son of man sitting at the right hand of Power [i.e. of God], and coming with the clouds of heaven" (Mk. xiv.62). Equally impossible is an appeal to the inscription on the cross: "The King of the Jews" (Mk. xv.26), for this was clearly inspired by the false charges brought against Jesus by His enemies (Lk. xxiii.1-5). If one thing stands out clearly, everywhere in the gospels, it is that Jesus was *not* a revolutionist, had no desire for earthly kingship (cf. Jn. vi.15; xviii.36), and could not have claimed Messiahship as it was commonly understood. If He accepted the title, it was only with reservations, or by reinterpretation, of which there is no hint in the gospels: and it seems far more likely that the title was conferred upon Him by the Church, which *did* reinterpret it. Even so, it was only a temporary title, and for Paul—i.e. for the Gentile churches as early as the year 49 or 50—it had ceased to be a title and had become part of a proper name: "Jesus Christ", or (more rarely) "Christ Jesus". So it is to this day: no one thinks of it as meaning "Jesus the Jewish Messiah", or "the Messiah Jesus". Christ is *not less, but far more*, than any earthly monarch, however idealised or "spiritualised", the ruler of one people, one nation, one tiny country in the Ancient World—and certainly far more than any monarch whose coronation, after all, never took place.

(*b*) The other title, "Son of Man", was also—as many

73

Christian scholars now believe—conferred on Jesus by the Church. It meant, undoubtedly, that He was to be the final judge of all mankind, as in Mt. xxv.31-46, or in the "Parables" of 1 Enoch (XXXVII-LXXI).

> This is the Son of Man who hath righteousness,
> With whom dwelleth righteousness,
> And who revealeth all the treasures of that
>   which is hidden. . . .
> And the sum of judgment was given unto the
>   Son of Man,
> And he caused the sinners to pass away
> And be destroyed from off the face of the earth
> And those who have led the world astray.
>
> (1 Enoch XLVI.3, LXIX.27)

The origin of the title is probably to be sought in Dan. VII.13 (*c.* 165 B.C.), where it is a symbolic figure, rather than in Ezek. II.1, III.1, etc., where it is used by God in addressing the lowly human prophet. In Dan. VII the "one like a son of man" (i.e. like a *human* being) is a striking contrast to the earlier beast-figures (vss. 2-8) which symbolised the great world-empires whose armies had ravaged and trodden down the earth; now at last was to come a humane world-rule, that of the Jews, which would follow the successful war of the Maccabees against the Seleucid empire. A century or more later, this symbolic figure was interpreted literally, as a description of *the* Son of Man in heaven, the heavenly Judge (not an earthly Messiah), who will destroy the wicked and punish "those who have led the world astray" (i.e. the wicked spirits).

But in the New Testament the term is used in a variety of ways. In St Mark's Gospel it is used paradoxically, as in the three Passion Announcements (VIII.31, IX.31, X.32f): the glorious Son of Man, who belongs in heaven (cf. Acts VII.56), must die here on earth! In Jn. XII.34 there is a puzzled note: the crowd in Jerusalem cannot decipher the

cryptic reference, and they ask, "Who is this Son of man?"
For it was indeed a puzzle: in ordinary Aramaic "son of
man" meant simply "a human being", while "*this* son of
man" was a way of designating oneself without saying
"I" (cf. the French *cet homme*). Whether or not the
populace of Jerusalem was familiar with the apocalyptic
figure (in I Enoch) may be questioned; some scholars hold
that I Enoch was post-Christian in date, or even a Christian
writing in origin. That Jesus used the term in reference
to Himself seems indubitable; but that He used it with
the connotations found in I Enoch—that is a question
upon which experts are divided, and no decisive evidence,
on one side or the other, has yet been discovered. It may
be doubted that Jesus used a term which was meant only
to baffle and frustrate His own followers, as well as all
His other hearers. That seems just as improbable as the
theory that His parables were designed to conceal His
teaching, as a hidden "mystery" (Mk. IV.11f). In fact,
the two theories, as interpretations of Jesus' character
and mission, probably belong together, and were designed
to support each other. Mark's theory of the "Messianic
secret" was possibly invented by Gentile Christians, for
whom truth was most naturally conceived as disguised or
hidden in paradox or mystery.

It is of course quite true that all these terms and titles
may be explained as used or at least suggested by Jesus
Himself, rather than by the later Church—though the
latter view is the simpler. If so, then each text, each title,
each application of a title must be separately explained,
often with a certain amount of reinterpretation or reserve,
since its full connotations would not be felt by Jesus's
hearers, either by the disciples, or by the crowds which
followed Him, or by His enemies who would have seized
upon them. This system of explanation is like the old
Ptolemaic astronomy, with its vast concentric circles, its
cycles and epicycles, each separate motion of every

celestial body being explained by some special force, cause, or motion. In the end, Copernicus arrived on the scene, revived the great, simple, all-inclusive theory of Aristarchus of Samos, who put the sun in the centre of the skies, not the earth, and then every celestial motion became clear. Protestant theology still awaits its Copernican revolution, when Christ shall be set at the centre—in place of a complicated system of various Christological views, titles, and concepts. These titles were only the Church's attempt to describe Him, to account for Him, for His personality, His mission and His work, His gracious teaching, His incomparably close relation to God, His ineffable, indescribable gentleness and power, the transforming magic of His influence, the mystery of His death and resurrection, His divinity and His humanity —in a word, "the mystery of Christ" (Eph. III.4). Every one of the titles ascribed to Him, as the Church proceeded to "crown him with many crowns", is rich and beautiful but inadequate. Even taken all together, they are only our poor human effort to describe and to account for one who, by every testimony, was totally unique. It is not the titles that explain Him; it is He who gives meaning to the titles. None of them is now used by the Church in its original sense, but with a transformed, transfigured meaning which reflects something more of "the glory of the Lord".

The Life of Jesus

No one doubts that Jesus really existed. The "Christ myth" school of fifty years ago is now totally extinct. "Is not this the carpenter, the son of Mary and brother of James and Joses and Judas and Simon, and are not his sisters here with us?" (Mk. VI.3)—this question should have answered the inquiry before it arose. The presupposition of the gospel tradition as a whole is the fact that Jesus lived, taught, performed miracles of healing and exorcism in Galilee, in the days of the tetrarch Herod Antipas, and died in Jerusalem on the false charge of fomenting revolution, under the procurator Pontius Pilate, about Passover time in the year 29 or 30. It is true, the story of His life has been embellished with certain miraculous incidents, of the kind always to be expected in an oral biographical tradition in the Ancient World. But, as also in such traditions, these had as a rule some foundation in fact, and at the heart of even the most highly developed anecdote there is usually a kernel of historical reminiscence—though history, or biography, was certainly not what the evangelists were trying to write. Their subject was the Gospel (Mk. 1.1), *the proclamation of the good news of salvation in and through Jesus Christ, the Son of God*. To this end, the stories were told and retold, as they had been told from the beginning of the Christian movement—including Jesus's own stories, His exquisitely beautiful and penetrating parables. That He exorcised demons and healed the sick is simply indubitable. His own explanation of what this meant is found in Mt. xii.28 and Lk. xi.20 (cf. Mt. xi.2-6), as we have already seen. It meant that God's Kingdom was already on the way, already in process of realisation or establishment, since the powers of darkness were now being rolled back in defeat. It was no "far-off divine event" at the distant end of history. It had already begun to be realised—here in Galilee! Jesus probably did not claim to be Messiah, King of Israel, God's vicegerent in the Age to Come; but He certainly acted as God's *agent* here and now, so that men inevitably thought also of Him when they thought of the full realisation, here or hereafter, of the Reign of God.

His calling of the disciples and His appointment of them (the Twelve), His teaching of the multitude and His training of His close personal disciples, His "ethics" of the Kingdom, His Transfiguration in a moment of vision on a lonely mountain-top, His Triumphal Entry into Jerusalem—all these and many more incidents and features in His Life and Ministry find their proper setting and perspective in the career of the One who was called and commissioned (Mk. 1.9-11) as God's agent or representative in the working out of His purposes. We describe it as "Messianic"; but it is "Messianic" only in the Christian sense. No one hitherto had dreamed of a Messiah who was a wandering prophet and teacher, a healer and exorcist; in brief, no one had dreamed of such a person as Jesus.

The stories of His birth, found in the later gospels, Luke (i-ii) and Matthew (i-ii), but nowhere else in the New Testament, are designed to explain His unique character and powers. As many scholars now believe, the story of the Annunciation to Mary, in Lk. 1.26-38, reads even more naturally without the "gloss" in vs. 34, "since I have no husband"—an impossible addition, since she was already betrothed to Joseph (vs. 27) and would soon be married. (Cf. the gloss in Lk. iii.23, "as was supposed.") The angel's answer (vs. 35) explains, not how she will have a son, but how her son will be qualified to receive the title and obtain the throne as described in vss. 32f—a purely nationalistic Messianic conception. Hence some scholars believe the "gloss" (if it is that) in vs. 34 is due to the influence of the text of Mt. 1.23 upon the text of Luke, at some date after the latter gospel had left its author's hands. In Matthew, the story is a "midrash," or fanciful explanation, of Is. vii.14 in the Greek translation (the word for "virgin" is not in the Hebrew text); and this, as many now believe, was the origin of the doctrine of the Virgin Birth, a beautiful imaginative story based upon an Old Testament text, full of meaning for the first century, full of difficulty for the twentieth. One need not reject it, any more than one need accept it. It is not a "saving" doctrine, i.e. one which is "necessary to salvation". It is "congruous" with the Incarnation, as theologians say, but the Incarnation—God's self-manifestation in a human life—does not depend upon it.

The story of the Virgin Birth belongs to the *poetry* of religion, and its proper place is in Christian art and devotion, not in theology. As some of the old Italian painters represented the scene of the Annunciation, Mary was kneeling before an open Bible; the passage she was reading was undoubtedly the ninth chapter of Isaiah, as the words of the angel entered her inmost soul, "*He* will be great . . . the Son of the Most High . . . and of *his* kingdom there will be no end" (Lk. 1.32-35)—Why not? Undoubtedly, following her prospective marriage she would bear a son; and why should not he be the one to fulfil the ancient divine promises, free his people, and rule over them forever in righteousness and peace? (See Lk. 1.36-55.) We Protestants are not much given to Mariolatry, and we really do not need to move in that direction in order to recognise that back of Jesus was his Mother, or that back of His conception of the Kingdom of God was the home in Nazareth where He grew up, or that back of all His teaching were the holy books of the Old Testament, which He had read and heard read from His childhood. Undoubtedly He was reared in an atmosphere of piety, like that described in Lk. i-ii. This may—as some think—be only a fantasy, but I think it is something more. I believe that in these opening chapters Luke is telling us something which is indispensable if we are to understand the divine-human character of the strong yet gracious Son of God who walked this earth in Galilee, the gentle One who was also the all-powerful, the utterly self-effacing One who was also the all-commanding, all-compelling, ever-attractive Saviour of mankind. And I am sure that this is how Luke thought of Him, for he says it on almost every page.

5

The Holy Spirit and the Church

The Beginnings of the Church

DEAN Joseph Barry of Nashotah House used to say that the Christian Church ought to erect "altars of reparation" to the Holy Spirit, as an amend for long centuries of neglect. Very few Christians, very few groups of Christians seem to take seriously the New Testament teaching about the Spirit. But there is no question that our religious belief and practice would be far stronger if we took the Holy Spirit in earnest. From beginning to end (Mt. 1.18; Rev. xxviii.17), the New Testament emphasises the Spirit's activity. We have already seen (in Chapter 2) the frequent references in Luke and Acts; indeed, as someone has said, the Acts of the Apostles might well be called "Acts of the Holy Spirit," for its action assumes that the early Church was Spirit-filled, Spirit-guided, Spirit-controlled. The great "outpouring" on the Day of Pentecost, described in Acts ii, is "programmatic" and constitutive, as Acts 1.4f, 8, and also Lk. xxiv.49 affirm. And yet it is not said that Pentecost was the "birthday" of the Church. For the Church, the New Israel, is continuous with the Old Israel, and therefore dates from Abraham and Moses (cf. Rom. iv.1; Gal. iii.6-9, 29; 1 Cor. x.1-4). As there was an outpouring of the Spirit at the giving of the Law (Num. xi.24-30), so there was another at the proclamation of the Gospel. As the older dispensation had prophets, priests, and seers who were "anointed" with the Spirit, as was also the architect of the tabernacle (Ex. xxxi.3, xxxv.31), so the new dispensation was likewise a "dispensation of the Spirit" (ii Cor. iv.8). It is a great mistake to assume that the Old Testament and Judaism knew nothing of the Holy Spirit. On the contrary, the New Testament takes it for granted that the Holy Spirit was already known in earlier times, and views the fresh Christian manifestation as a renewal. Thus both Old Testament and New reflect the "religion of the Spirit". Jesus Himself is viewed as possessed by—or possessing—the Holy Spirit; only, whereas others received a limited measure of the divine gift, He had received it "not by measure" (Jn. iii.34), i.e. without limit. This gift He has passed on to His disciples, according to the same gospel (Jn. xx.22). Not only was His earthly Ministry of exorcism, healing, teaching, and remission of sins the activity of the Holy Spirit (Acts x.38), but His death and Resurrection were "in the Spirit" (see Acts i.2; i Tim. iii.16). "Through the eternal Spirit [he] offered himself . . . to God" (Heb. ix.14), and by His Resurrection "in the Spirit" or "by the Spirit" He obtained the power to raise others with Him, through union with Him, and to "justify" them in the presence of God (i Tim. iii.16). The cross was not, according to the New Testament, a lonely gibbet on a hill outside Jerusalem where an innocent man was once put to a shameful death; it was the battlefield where the powerful Lord Christ had met and vanquished the demonic powers that were bent on His annihilation, and had triumphed over them openly (Col. ii.15)—an idea which the early Church continued to ponder for a long time, but which was forgotten when legalistic theories of the atonement came in with the fifth and later centuries.

Nor was the Resurrection the mere resuscitation or reanimation of a dead body—like that of Lazarus or the boy at Nain or Jairus's daughter or the corpse laid on the prophet's bones in the days of the Syrian border wars

(Jn. xi.44; Lk. vii.15; Mk. v.42; ii Kings xiii.21). We misinterpret the Resurrection, and only create insuperable difficulties for ourselves and others, when we talk about Christ's rising "from the grave" or "from the tomb"; the New Testament describes it as "from the dead"—and that means "*from among* the dead" (*ek tōn nekrōn*), as one singled out from among the many departed in the other world (see i Cor. xv.12, 20; Eph. v.14; Col. 1.18; i Thess. 1.10; Heb. xiii.20; Gospel acc. to the Hebrews, frag. quoted by Jerome, *Illustrious Men*, §2, *a dormientibus*). Naturally language is flattened down in time; the earliest language was far more vivid, and reflected the earliest beliefs far more accurately than the later. The earliest statements affirm that Christ "was raised" (i.e. by God; *ēgeiren*, Acts iii.15, iv.10, etc.); later He is described as "rising" by His own power: "he rose again" (*anestē*, as in i Thess. iv.14 and in the Creed). As in St John's Gospel, "I have power to lay it [my life] down, and I have power to take it again" (Jn. x.18).

In the very earliest of all references to the Resurrection, apart from the oral tradition underlying the gospels, viz. in the list of appearances in i Cor. xv.4-8, Paul says that in his preaching he had stressed the fact that Christ died and was raised and had "appeared" to His disciples—last of all to Paul himself. The word for "appear" is the technical one used in the Old Testament (i.e. in the Greek translation), *ōphthē*, which describes an objectively real yet spiritual manifestation. One does not just happen to see God or an angel—as Achilles caught a glimpse of his divine mother on the battlefield before Troy. If a divine or supernatural being is seen at all, it is because that divine being chooses to be seen, and so "manifests" himself to the viewer. When Christ was "seen" by the Apostles, He "appeared to" them, as the r.s.v. correctly translates.

The later accounts tend to stress the corporeality of the Resurrection: for example the empty tomb (Mk. xvi.6);

or the tangibility of Christ's body (Lk. xxiv.40; Jn.xx.27—
a clear refutation of the statements in the Gnostic "Acts
of John"); or the eating of food (Acts x.41; though neither
Lk. xxiv.30 nor Jn. xxi.13 says that Jesus himself ate—
the language is eucharistic, as in Lk. xxii.19). But the
earliest conception was of a spiritual body, raised in or by
the Holy Spirit, and manifesting itself visibly—not to all
men, but to "chosen witnesses" (Acts x.41). Christ then
became, outwardly and visibly, the Son of God, the
heavenly Messiah: as Paul says, He was "designated Son
of God in power according to the Spirit of holiness [the
Holy Spirit] by his resurrection from the dead"—(Rom.
1.4; "according to the Spirit" matches "according to the
flesh" in vs. 3: the new divine status is superior to the
earlier human). For "Christ being raised from the dead
will never die again; death no longer has dominion over
him" (Rom. vi.9). If the believer is to have a "new" and
glorious body, at the Resurrection (1 Cor. xv.35-50),
certainly the Lord had likewise been raised up and
glorified; His body was no mere reanimation or transformation of a body of "flesh and blood", but was transcendent, spiritual, incorruptible.

Along with the later emphasis on the physical reality
of Christ's Resurrection—an emphasis which was natural,
perhaps even necessary and inevitable, when the Church
found itself face to face with Gnosticism—the question of
the final disappearance, or rather of the *last* appearance,
of the heavenly Christ was answered by the story of the
Ascension, found only in Luke-Acts. The other gospels do
not mention it, and the Epistle to Hebrews assumes that
Christ went directly from the cross to His state of glory
in heaven (Heb. iv.14, viii.1, ix.12). Even St John's
Gospel, in places, speaks of the Cross as if it were the point
of Christ's exaltation (Jn. xii.32), and as if His reappear-
ance on earth (described in Jn. xx-xxi) was only incidental
and took place in order to convince the doubting minds of

Thomas and others. The central affirmation of the New Testament is that Christ's death, Resurrection, and glorification was an action, one and continuous, which was of cosmic importance, and that essentially it took place in the invisible or spiritual world. Only its echoes, only its after-effects and consequences, were audible or visible in this world, and then only to the select few, the faithful disciples and Paul. How very different is the earliest New Testament conception from the popular idea, in later and in modern times, of the reanimation or restoration to life again of Jesus's physical body, as a proof of "the immortality of the soul"! These two ideas, the ancient and the modern, do not conflict: they do not even intersect, they never come near each other, they move on totally different levels!

Very naturally, the "spiritual" atmosphere of the early Church was strong and positive. Not only have modern psychologists studied the mind of Christ and tried to show that He was a mystic, a visionary, with a "spiritual" or "pneumatic" personality, but the same tests have been applied to the Apostles. There are scholarly German "psychographies" (studies of the inner soul) of both Peter and Paul, treating them as "ecstatics," for whom the invisible world was more real than the visible, and who were not only, like the author of the Apocalypse, "in the Spirit on the Lord's day" (Rev. 1.10), but on all other days as well. But the theory goes too far. Paul himself refers to the "spiritual" experiences which he has enjoyed (e.g. II Cor. XII.1-10) and he acknowledges that he also "speaks in tongues" (I Cor. XIV.18); but he adds, "I would rather speak five words with my mind, in order to instruct others, than ten thousand words in a tongue" (I Cor. XIV.19). His whole emphasis was upon the practical side of the religious life, not these extravagant emotional displays.

The worship of the early Church was also "spiritual"

(Rom. XII.1). It is sometimes thought that the picture of the early Christian congregation in Corinth, reflected in 1 Corinthians, was typical of the whole Church. But this is certainly not true. For one thing, the epistles of the New Testament, which are addressed to Christian congregations, and also the gospels, the homilies, even the Book of Revelation, are full of references to Scripture—echoes, allusions, overtones, as well as quotations—which it is assumed the recipients or hearers will recognise. Accordingly the place of Scripture-reading and exposition in Christian worship must have been far greater than 1 Corinthians seems to imply. Further, when the Church emerges from its second-century "tunnel" (the obscure period for which only slight literary evidence has survived), the liturgy, its prayers and order of service, and even the offices and titles of the ministry, are almost all taken over from the Jewish synagogue. It seems far more likely that the normal Christian service of worship was Scripture-centred, like the service in the synagogue, and that lessons ("lections"), prayers, psalms and hymns, with exposition of Scripture or homilies, were part of the normal order of procedure. The Lord's Prayer as given in Mt. VI.9-13 was surely a form used in public worship (it is also found in the second-century Didache, VIII.2); and it has close contacts with one of the most ancient Jewish prayers, still used in the Jewish synagogue. With this agrees the picture of the earliest Church in Acts. Although the Apostles were "filled with the Holy Spirit and began to speak in other tongues, as the Spirit gave them utterance" (Acts II.4), their converts promptly "devoted themselves to the apostles' teaching and fellowship, to the breaking of bread and the prayers" (Acts II.42) —presumably the prayers said in the synagogue. Eight verses later on (Acts III.1), Peter and John are described as going up to the Temple "at the hour of prayer, the ninth hour" (three p.m.). It is inconceivable that a serious

85

body of Christian Jews, assembled for divine worship, could have indulged ordinarily in the wild, ecstatic worship reflected in 1 Corinthians—or that the Corinthians themselves could always have worshipped God in this extravagant, purely emotional, corybantic fashion.

Our earliest evidence—as we have seen in Chapter 4—indicates that the early Church in Palestine addressed prayers to Christ: the *Marana tha* ("Our Lord, come!") of 1 Cor. xvi.22 is an Aramaic ejaculation—and Aramaic was the popular language of Palestine. The Lord Jesus Himself was even described as Spirit, or a spirit, or the Spirit (cf. ii Cor. iii.17)—at least, as the one who *sends* the Holy Spirit (Acts ii.33). And when it is assumed, as in 1 Cor. xiv.26-33 and in Jn. xv.13, that further revelations will be made, it is because both the exalted Christ and the Holy Spirit are present in the Church, inspiring fresh utterances of divine revelation. Thus although revelation was complete in Christ (Jn. 1.16-18), it was Christ Himself who was inspiring these further expressions. The new words were coming from Him—as to the churches in the Province of Asia in Rev. i-iii, where they are both messages from the exalted, heavenly Christ and also "what the Spirit says to the churches" (Rev. ii.29).

The Sacraments

Such was the atmosphere of the early Church—one of intense spiritual exaltation or "elation." The New Age was expected to come at once, in fact to be already in process of arrival. Already the presence of the risen Christ and the Holy Spirit was so real and so powerful that unbelievers, persecutors, and liars could be struck blind, dumb, or dead (as Acts v.1-14, viii.19, ix.9, xiii.11). The very air was charged with the supernatural, and coming events were invisibly but powerfully moving into their place in the scheme of things. The "powers of the Age to Come" (Heb. vi.5) were already being manifested, and

86

before long their full realisation would be obvious to all men. It was in such an atmosphere that the earliest Christians lived, thought, prayed, pondered the Scriptures, taught, and testified to their faith. The ethos and background of the Sacraments and also of the earliest formulations of Christian belief are to be found in this tense conviction of "realised eschatology"—not in some more modernly conceived atmosphere of theological discussion, memorial observance, or well-planned programme for church activities or evangelism. The early Church was on fire with its convictions!

The Sacrament of *Baptism* was undoubtedly observed from the first (see Acts ii.41). The question, when was the rite adopted by the Church? is to be answered accordingly: it never was "adopted", since it was in use from the very beginning. Its origin no doubt goes back to John the Baptiser, many of whose followers became Christians (as in Acts xix.1-7; Jn. 1.35-51). In fact, "the beginning of the Gospel" was commonly thought to date from John and his preaching of baptism (Acts x.37). Jesus Himself had received John's baptism and had probably shared his religious movement—though it is a mistake to suppose that either Jesus or John was an Essene or a member of the sect at Qumran which produced the "Dead Sea Scrolls". At Qumran, "baptism" meant frequent, perhaps daily lustrations; for John, as all the gospels, the book of Acts, and Josephus agree in showing, baptism was a once-for-all self-immersion for cleansing and dedication to a new life.

In Mark 1.4, it is said that John preached "a baptism of repentance for the forgiveness of sins". That means a baptism which was *motivated* by repentance and was *intended to* effect, or *to be the means of*, the removal of sins. Our word "forgiveness" is usually adequate to translate the Greek word *aphesis*, but the realism of ancient religion requires something more like the Authorised Version word "remission". We can say that we "forgive" a debt; but the usual word is "cancel". We can "remit" a debt— but that is most unusual; we "remit" money. Languages always change, and if English has changed in 350 years, since the Authorised Version of 1611, how much more has the understanding of first-century Greek! Sins are not merely unfulfilled obligations which God can—and does— cancel, but they are positive contaminations with evil which must be cleansed and washed away. As we have seen (Chapter 3), what is required is not only (1) forgiveness (a personal act) for past sins (which were personal offences against God), but also (2) cleansing from their pollution, and (3) the power to "go and sin no more". Hence baptism, the rite of cleansing and initiation, does something more than insure forgiveness. Although the New Testament accounts of John's baptism probably tend to describe it in later (i.e. in Christian) terms, they clearly recognise (Mk. 1.8; Lk. III.16; Acts 1.5) one very important distinction: Christian Baptism conferred the Spirit—it was a "baptism with the Holy Spirit" as well as "with water" (Jn. III.5). In time it came to be recognised (as here in John) that Baptism was even more than this: it meant regeneration, the beginning of the new life in Christ, the spiritual "rebirth" which transformed an "unregenerate" person into "a child of God, a member of Christ, and an inheritor of the Kingdom of Heaven". Of course this additional language was not the result of theological speculation, but of Christian experience, under the tremendous impact of the new and vitalising power which was felt to be present in the Church (see Heb. VI.1-6). As Paul stated it, in mystical language, the Christian died with Christ, was buried with Him in Baptism, rose with Him in the likeness of His Resurrection (cf. Rom. VI.1-4), and therefore shared in the "new being" which Christ had achieved by His victory over death and His exaltation at God's right hand (cf. Rom. VI.5-11; Col. III.1-3).

The *Supper of the Lord* has been similarly viewed, by some, as a rite "adopted" (perhaps following one of Paul's "visions," I Cor. XI.23-26) as a memorial of the death of Christ. But, again, this rite was also clearly coeval with the Church: if "the prayers" in Acts II.42 were those of the Christian synagogue, taken over from the Jewish, including the ancient Shema ("Hear, O Israel") and the Benedictions said twice daily by every faithful Jew, then certainly "the breaking of bread" (literally "the" bread) was the sacred Christian fellowship meal observed from the beginning, and taken over, originally, from the holy meals observed by pious Jews. Among the Pharisees these were a part of the *Kiddush* or "sanctification" of the approaching holy day or Sabbath, when devout persons gathered to read and study the Scriptures, meditate upon them and share in their exposition, after which they concluded with prayers and a simple meal of bread and wine. Presumably this was the character of Jesus's last supper with His disciples (as well as of their earlier meals together), though here the overtones of the approaching Passover are clearly to be heard.

If John's chronology is correct, the Last Supper *preceded* the Passover, and was not identical with it, as the Synoptic Gospels assume. But in either case the Passover set the tone: see Paul's words in I Cor. V.7, and compare Lk. XXII.15f (in I Cor. XI.23-26 the Passover is not mentioned, nor is it mentioned in most Christian liturgies, to this day). What Jesus clearly did, at the Last Supper, was to bind His disciples to Himself by an indissoluble bond, as real as the "blood covenant" in the desert, a sharing in His own life, His body and His blood. Come now what might, whether defeat and death or victory and a triumph, Jesus and His disciples were henceforth inseparably *one*. It is not unlikely that Jesus expected the disciples to die with Him—if the result turned out to be His death. That He expected crucifixion is not certain (the predictions in

the Passion announcements, in Mk. VIII.31, etc., are mod-
elled on the Passion narrative); He may have expected
death by stoning, the Jewish penalty—if He was to die at
all. The ethos of those last hours in the Upper Room was
like that of the final meal before a commando raid or the
flight of a squadron which was being sent on some forlorn
but indispensable mission. They might meet again, but
not all would be present. Perhaps none would ever come
back—at least not to the Upper Room! But meet again
they would, Jesus insisted, when He took the cup and
vowed, "I shall not drink again of this fruit of the vine until
that day when I drink it new with you in my Father's
kingdom" (Mt. XXVI.29).

In the early Church, in the later Church, and also today, the Supper has meant many things to different
Christians, to many different groups of people. The highly
mystical, supernatural interpretation given it in Jn. VI
and in the great Catholic tradition is one type of Christian
religious belief. The social interpretation, as a fellowship
of consecration; the memorial emphasis, and also the
eschatological—both of which Paul stressed (I Cor. XI.26);
the sacrificial, deeply rooted in the Roman liturgy and in
some others; the closer connexion with the Resurrection
and the new life in Christ, which is stressed in the "holy
mysteries" of the Eastern churches; the emphasis upon
sin and forgiveness, the fresh access of grace, the joyful
renewal of communion and fellowship with Christ Himself, seen in the Lutheran, Anglican, and certain other
liturgies—all these emphases, including the doctrine of
the "real presence" (for surely here Christ is present, if
anywhere in the world!) go back to that Upper Room,
and to the later gatherings of the Jewish Christians as
they "broke bread from house to house" (cf. Acts II.46
A.V.). Like Baptism, all this is not the fruit of theological
speculation but of a rich, living experience, in closest contact with the Church's central tradition of the life of

Christ, and within the warm family fellowship of those who love and serve the Lord Jesus. Alas, that it has ever at any time been an occasion for argument, disputation, ostracism, excommunication, and severance of friendly relations between Christians! Today a new view is in the making, based partly upon a better understanding of the New Testament and of the Church itself, and partly upon a deeper and more sympathetic understanding of what religion means to other Christians, other groups than our own. If we are ever to realise the dream of a united "ecumenical" Church, it will have to include—some would say it will have to begin with—a new understanding and observance of the Holy Eucharist, one which is closer to its understanding and observance in the early Church.

The Ministry

The same is true of the New Testament view of the Christian ministry. There was not just one and only one valid type of ministry in the first century, but a variety of types. As Paul insisted, "there are varieties of gifts, but the same Spirit" (1 Cor. xii.4-31). These ministrations— or ministries—included apostleship, prophecy, teaching, reading, healing, exorcism, speaking with tongues, interpretation of tongues, the administration of charity, the care of the poor, and still other activities which characterised the small scattered congregations here and there throughout the eastern half of the Roman Empire. In time, three types of ministry stood out as normal: "bishops, presbyters, and deacons." But even so, other ministries were recognised, e.g. that of the deaconess.

At first the Apostles were the "centres of unity", and their qualifications included not only a divine call and commission, and the obvious possession of—or by—the Holy Spirit, but also the fact that they had "seen the Lord" (Acts 1.22; 1 Cor. ix.1). But even the Apostles could not be everywhere at once, any more than modern bishops or other clergymen can be! Paul wrote many letters; but these were an unsatisfactory substitute for personal visits, as he himself observed (1 Cor. xi.34b). Special representatives, Timothy, Titus, and others, were sent to represent him; but even this was not enough. Eventually, as we see from the Pastoral Epistles (i-ii Tim.; Tit.), settled leaders and heads of churches were required, who could exercise oversight of the Church's internal affairs and also represent the Church to the world outside. The day soon came when this was tragically true: the bishop had to be "God's athlete", strong and prepared to face martyrdom, and never to yield, whatever the provocation, under torture or threat of death. These men also, as the early Christian literature makes clear, were conscious of possession by the Spirit, and of special guidance, calling, and resources. Ignatius of Antioch, Polycarp of Smyrna, not to mention Peter and Paul and the earlier martyrs of the New Testament period, were consciously "Spirit-filled, Spirit-guided" men. The gospels themselves reflect the belief that their testimony, under persecution, would be inspired: "Settle it therefore in your minds, not to meditate beforehand how to answer; for I will give you a mouth and wisdom, which none of your adversaries will be able to withstand or contradict" (Lk. xxi.14f) —"the Holy Spirit will teach you in that very hour what you ought to say" (Lk.xii.12). Matthew goes even farther: "it is not you who speak [in giving your testimony when persecuted], but the Spirit of your Father speaking through you" (Mt. x.20; cf. Acts vii.55).

This was the atmosphere, the ethos, the outlook of the Church in the days when the Christian ministry took shape—it was a Spirit-guided function from the first (see Acts xiii.2f). Much of our difficulty, in current "ecumenical" discussions, is that we still think of the ministry as planned in advance by Jesus, who must have outlined the functions of the various orders, and then committed to the Apostles—or to Peter (Mt. xvi.17-19)—the responsibility for organising and administering the Church as an institution destined to survive for ages. This view was perfectly natural at the Reformation, and in the Middle Ages, and in the days of the Church Fathers; its beginnings can be traced even in the Gospel of Matthew, where rules are laid down for procedure in church courts and where the exalted Christ promises to be with His Church "to the close of the age" (Mt. xxviii.20). But the earlier writings in the New Testament are all but unanimous in suggesting that the ministry arose in response to immediate needs, in a highly-charged atmosphere of eschatological expectation and under the immediate guidance of the Holy Spirit. Perhaps the Spirit's guidance is still needed for the solution of our problems today, for example, such problems as the validity or authority of the ministry, or its sacramental function and office. Surely that guidance is far more desperately needed, for the facing of the manifold problems of our day, than most of us have begun to realise.

Like Baptism and the Lord's Supper, so also the ministry was dependent upon the Jewish pattern of community organisation. The "elders" were not specially-designated religious officers, but were simply the heads of the community, who functioned religiously—e.g. in handling the affairs of the synagogue—as they did elsewhere. When the Apostles "appointed elders for them in every church, with prayer and fasting" (Acts xiv.23), they were not necessarily ordaining clergymen; but it was out of this "setting apart" for a special office and responsibility in the Christian community that ordination arose, under the guidance, as we believe, of the Holy Spirit. Not only the title, "presbyter" (elder), but also the function was taken over from Judaism, though in the course of time this naturally grew and changed, as the Church faced new conditions in new and different places.

The Apostles' teaching (*didachē*: *doctrina*: teaching), which
is emphasised in the ideal picture of Acts II.42, undoubtedly
included the basic teachings of Judaism, namely the one-
ness and sovereignty of God, His requirement of righteousness and justice, His purpose of salvation and His plan
for the Judgment and the coming New Age. But this
teaching also undoubtedly included the teaching of Jesus,
as well as the fact of His resurrection and the change which
this had made in the relations between men and God. It
is astonishing to some readers to find how little "theology"
and how much "ethics" the New Testament contains,
especially in the teaching of Jesus—at least as reported in
the earlier or Synoptic Gospels. (John is different, and
confronts a theological situation created by Docetic
Gnosticism.) Almost every epistle ends with "practical"
admonitions, and one of them—James—is almost wholly
ethical.

The question, whether or not these ethics (e.g. the
Sermon on the Mount) can be put into practice, seems
never to have arisen. Only in our own time has a dark,
negative, pessimistic, really cynical view of human nature
arisen, with an equally discouraged view of the Gospel,
maintaining that the Sermon on the Mount set forth "an
impossible ideal", or sketched a "heroic" rule of life meant
only for martyrs during the interval of the "great tribulation" which was to precede the Last Judgment—the
"interim ethics" described by Albert Schweitzer. But the
theory is quite unhistorical, to say the least. Many of the
admonitions in the gospels have parallels in ancient
Jewish teaching. Was it ever supposed that this Jewish
teaching set too high, too heroic a standard, one much too
hard for human achievement, and therefore designed only
to force men to their knees in penitence and helplessness
and compel them to beg for mercy and divine grace? Not

according to these new theologians, who reject Judaism even more vigorously than they do the Gospel! Furthermore, how can we possibly close our eyes to the existence of saints who *have* achieved this high standard? or to the fact that, in the New Testament, all Christians are "called to be saints"?

But there is also "theology" in the New Testament, and even in the gospels. The *Atonement*, for example, is simply presupposed. "Christ died for our sins", as Paul insisted (i Cor. xv.3), and His death was not only a victory over Death, but also a removal of the burden of pollution and guilt which sin had entailed—not ours only, but the sin of the whole world (see Heb .i.3; i Jn. ii.2, iv.10). At first, no doubt, this was more or less only an explanation of why Christ had died—as the otherwise meaningless deaths of the martyrs were explained in ii Macc. vii.37f, iv Macc. vi.6, 29, ix.20, x.8, xvii.22, and elsewhere. It had been necessary ("the Son of man *must* suffer" Mk. viii.31), as part of God's plan, and God would surely bring to pass what He had intended. When the early Christians found, as a matter of deep personal experience, that their relations to God had actually changed, upon their acknowledgment of Christ as their Lord, this explanation of His death became obvious. All their lives they—like all other men in ancient times—had lived in a world where sacrifice was the natural and necessary condition of the removal of sin, its guilt, its pollution, its alienation from God, and where for thousands of years scarcely anyone had ever dreamed of any other mode of cleansing and restoration. What could have been more natural than to interpret this new experience of reconciliation with God, of release from sin and guilt, of cleansing from pollution, and of access of new power by which to live a life pleasing to God, than as an "Atonement" through the death of the Son of God? The *truth* of this doctrine does not lie in the realm of metaphysics, nor even in that of abstract

95

theology, but is rooted deeply in the living experience of men. It is still so rooted, to this day. And without that experience, the doctrine is meaningless, no matter in what theoretical form—ancient, medieval, or modern—the doctrine is presented. Furthermore, it is perfectly possible to believe in the Atonement, to accept and to experience it, without any theory to explain *how* it came about that "in Christ God was reconciling the world to himself" (II Cor. v.19 R.S.V. mg.) The initiative was God's, not man's, not even Christ's; and by it the world was being reconciled to God, not God to the world. These principles are all-important, and are decisive for the Christian understanding of the doctrine.

6

The Life of the World to Come

"Apocalyptic Eschatology"

IT is now generally recognised that an "eschatological" outlook dominated the early Church, not only in the New Testament period but for some time after. The beginning of the Gospel, in the days of John the Baptist, was Jesus's proclamation, "The time is fulfilled, and the kingdom of God is at hand; repent, and believe in the gospel," i.e. believe in this good news (Mk. 1.15). At the other end of the New Testament period, it is true, there were those whose love had begun to grow cold (Mt. xxiv. 12), while some complained, "Where is the promise of his coming? For ever since the fathers fell asleep, all things have continued as they were from the beginning of the creation" (II Pet. III.4). II Peter probably dates from *c.* A.D. 150; a half-century later Clement of Alexandria and Origen marked the complete abandonment of any expectation of the immediate coming of the Kingdom. But in between the days of John the Baptist and the latest New Testament book, the eschatological outlook and emphasis was all but universal. Jesus certainly expected the immediate coming—in fact, as we have seen, He believed that the "signs of the times" all pointed to the Kingdom as already on its way, and He expected that it would soon be fully manifested. The Apostles certainly held this view, and also the conviction that Jesus was the one who had fully realised the promises of God (II Cor. 1.20), and was now in Heaven, seated at God's right hand

(Eph. 1.20), from whence He would soon come and hold the Last Judgment of all mankind. Various conceptions of the Age to Come, and of the events to precede the end, were set forth in the New Testament writings; they exhibit much the same variety as that which is found in the Jewish apocalyptic writings of the same period, i.e. beginning with the Book of Daniel (c. 165 B.C.) and ending with II Esdras (=IV Ezra) and II Baruch (c. A.D. 100). Moreover the conception of the heavenly Son of Man, found in the "Parables" of I Enoch, is also taken for granted in parts of the New Testament (see Chapter 4 above). As Professor Ethelbert Stauffer and others maintain, "apocalyptic eschatology" was the closest and most natural background anywhere to be found in contemporary Judaism as the setting for the rise of Christian belief.

There are many who hold that Jesus Himself was an apocalyptist, and identified Himself with the heavenly Son of Man. Others believe that He was an eschatological prophet, but not an apocalyptist, and that the identification of the risen and glorified Jesus with the exalted Son of Man reflects the faith of the Church, not Jesus's own conviction. Whichever view is correct, one fact is certain: the "eschatological" outlook, as distinct from the "apocalyptic", characterises not only the New Testament but also the Old. As contrasted with the old Oriental religions, e.g. with Hinduism, and also with Graeco-Roman religion, the religion of the Hebrews and the Jews looked forward, not backward, to a Golden Age. It took for granted God's absolute sovereignty, His ability to control all events in heaven and earth and bend them to His purposes—He could make even "the wrath of man" to praise Him (Ps. LXXVI.10). Accordingly, the course of history *must* finally lead to the realisation of the divine plan. The Bible does not say that "all things" by their very nature "work together for good," but that "in every-

98

thing *God works* for good with those who love him" (Rom. VIII.28 R.S.V.).

It is this Hebrew and Jewish "eschatological" idea, this linear rather than circular view of history, which is also presupposed in the New Testament. The ancient prophetic conviction is still strong, namely that God is in absolute control of events, and nothing escapes Him; that nothing can frustrate His purposes; and that nothing can fail to serve its appointed end, in the final realisation upon earth of the divine Reign which exists—and has always existed—everywhere else in the universe. God's Kingdom is "everlasting" (Ps. CXLV.13), and yet by a paradox it must "come" here on earth. It will come, as Jesus said, when God's will is done "on earth as it is in heaven" (Mt. VI.10).

The difference between "apocalyptic" eschatology and "prophetic" is to be seen partly in the intensity of its conviction of the nearness of the end of history, the great turning-point soon to be reached, and partly in the methodical calculation of "times and seasons" (which Jesus repudiated, Acts I.7) and the working out of a rigid timetable or schedule for coming events—chiefly the un-fulfilled prophecies of the Old Testament. There was also a stronger strain of dualism in apocalyptic thought, and much more use was made of angels, demons, and other celestial *dramatis personae*; and there was a whole set of machinery, consisting of supernatural "signs, wonders, and portents" which the apocalyptists used in describing the approach of the end. By the very nature of the case, this additional apocalyptic element or emphasis added nothing to the religious meaning or exigency of the Gospel, but only made its acceptance burdensome for those who held a nonapocalyptic view of the world. It was only a temporary phase of thought, and in course of time it was left behind, its flaming manifestos thereafter being read as poetry, not prose, and certainly not as sober prediction of the future. It is curious that the Book of Revelation—the chief example of apocalyptic thought in the New Testament—was finally admitted to the New Testament Canon, i.e. included in the authoritative list of generally accepted contents, because it was understood to contain a preview of the future history of the Church. Other parts of the New Testament which reflect this apocalyptic strain of thought are found in I Thess. IV.13-V.11; II Thess. I.5-II.12, and especially in the "Little Apocalypse" now embedded in Mk. XIII (i.e. in vss. 6-8, 14-20, 24-27) and in the elaboration of Mark's apocalyptic chapter in Mt. XXIV-XXV. Many scholars hold that the apocalyptic element in this final discourse, i.e. its underlying basis in Mk. XIII, goes back to some early Christian Jewish "revelation", written perhaps in the year 40 when the crisis caused by Caligula's proposed erection of his own statue in the Temple convinced many persons that the last days had arrived (see especially Mk. XIII.14-16; Mt. XXIV.15-18; on the other hand, Lk. XXI.20-22 reinterprets this to mean the siege of Jerusalem in A.D. 68-70).

There were other apocalypses in circulation in the early Church. One, known as the *Apocalypse of Peter*, enjoyed considerable reputation for a time, but was finally shelved, as its reading at the Church's public services was prohibited in one area after another. The fragments of this writing that have come down to us prove it to have been more pagan than Jewish in character, and to have contained even less of the spirit of the Gospel than some parts of the *Apocalypse of John*, our Book of Revelation. Neither apocalypse is to be taken as a description of conditions or events in heaven or hell, but as a vast, panoramic, symbolic portrayal of what one seer (who however, quoted others) thought the course of events *here on earth* was to be like. In the Book of Revelation the vials, the trumpets, the beasts, the horned heads—all these are part of the equipment or "properties" of every apocalyptic writer, from Daniel down to the second Christian century—with a few odd survivals or revivals in later centuries, both in Judaism and Christianity. The great central teaching of the Book of Revelation is not this prognostication of the future—which failed, as all such prognostications have always failed—but its profound convictions which underlie all these gaudy stage-settings: (*a*) that God is in absolute control of events, despite the persecution of the faithful, and the threatened extinction of the churches in the Province of Asia; and (*b*) that the souls of the martyrs and of all who "die in the Lord" are in bliss, safe in the presence of their heavenly Master and His Christ, who is about to conquer the nations and make them His Kingdom (Rev. xi.15).

The Revelation of John is clearly a "pamphlet for hard times", as someone once described the Book of Daniel. It was written, as St Irenaeus (*c.* A.D. 185) said—or rather, as he said, "it was seen"—"almost in our own generation, toward the end of the reign of the Emperor Domitian," probably *c.* A.D. 95 (*Against Heresies*, v.30.3). Addressed to the Christians in the rich and populous province where the Roman imperial cultus had taken deepest root, and where enthusiastic chambers of commerce (the provincial "assemblies") were promoting emperor-worship for the sake of trade, the Apocalypse could easily have been viewed as a proclamation of rebellion against the Empire. Only the weapons of this revolt—"the weapons of our warfare" as Paul had called them (ii Cor. x.4)—were not swords and javelins but prayers and supplications, the testimony of martyrs, and the "good word" of God to the persecuted faithful. The author certainly looks forward to the fall of Rome (Rev. xvii-xix), and to the final realisation upon earth of the Kingdom of God, when Christ shall reign for a thousand years—as Papias and others interpreted Rev. xx; but he also looks upward to the unshakable foundations of the heavenly city, already existing (Rev. IV, V, VII, XI), where the martyrs are in peace; and he also looks forward to the final realisation, "in the end and beyond the end", as James Moffatt used to say, of the "new heaven" and "new earth" in which righteousness dwells (Rev. xx-xxi). Then at last "the tabernacle of God" will be "with men", and "they shall be his people, and God himself will be with them" (Rev. xxi.3f A.V.).

It is probably this fundamental conviction which has endeared the book to countless Christian readers, not only in the days of persecution but at all times. There is no finer poem on the life to come than the one in Rev. VII. 15-17. Those who have come out of great tribulation are the martyrs; they have washed their robes and made them white in the blood of the Lamb (note the age-old motif of purification, once more, now to be realised after death):

> Therefore are they before the throne of God,
> and serve him day and night within his temple;
> and he who sits upon the throne will shelter them
> with his presence.
> They shall hunger no more, neither thirst any more;
> the sun shall not strike them, nor any scorching heat.
> For the Lamb in the midst of the throne will be their
> shepherd,
> and he will guide them to springs of living water;
> and God will wipe away every tear from their eyes.
> (Rev. VII.15-17)

"The Lamb" is the victorious, risen, glorified Christ who has gone forth "conquering and to conquer" and who will in the end bring all nations to serve the true God. The name may be a cryptogram, like the "number" of the "beast" in Rev. XIII.18, where "666" (or "616," the variant reading mentioned by Irenaeus) clearly means "Nero Caesar"—and also, perhaps, "Domitian"! Or it is like the symbolic fish, *Ichthus* ("Jesus Christ Son of God Saviour"), used by the early Roman Christians in the catacombs and mentioned by Abercius in his mortuary inscription at Hieropolis in Phrygia (*c.* 70 miles NE. of Laodicea), not far away from the churches to which the Apocalypse was sent. For the word for "lamb", used twenty-eight times in the Book of Revelation, is somewhat unusual: *Arnion*, not *Amnos* (which is used in Jn. 1.29, 36). One wonders if it could have been preferred for its value as an acrostic, something perhaps like this: *Autos* (he) or *Autous* (them) '*Rabdō* (with a rod) *Nikēsei* (he will conquer)—*Iēsous* (Jesus) '*O* (the) *Nazōraios* (Nazoraean) or *Nazarēnos* (Nazarene). Certainly Ps. ii.8f was one of the author's favourite texts (see Rev. ii.27, xii.5, xix.15), and his conception of the victorious Lamb of God is only faintly hinted in the favourite altar decoration of the old painters, a pure white lamb bearing the banner of victory over one shoulder.

Resurrection and Eternal Life

It is a widespread idea at the present time that Christian teaching insists upon the "resurrection of the body" as opposed to the "immortality of the soul", and rejects the latter as merely a pagan speculation. The "Biblical" doctrine is resurrection, pure and simple, and appeal is made to Paul (1 Cor. xv) in support of the statement. But this sweeping generalisation is not wholly true: the Bible also teaches immortality. In the Old Testament the "primitive" conception of Sheōl is practically the same as the Greek idea of Hades: a vast cavernous realm beneath the earth where the souls or "shades" of the dead are gathered and live on for an indefinite period in the gloom. It was a realm far removed from the sunlit upper earth, and far from God's presence. There men could not even worship Him.

> The dead do not praise the Lord,
> nor do any that go down into silence.
>
> (Ps. cxv.17)

These lines match Homer's preference: Better it is to be a serf upon earth, even to an impoverished master, than to reign over all the dead! (*Odyssey* xi.488-491; see p. 57). But as time went on, religious men and women became convinced that even here God must be known, loved, and worshipped.

> Whither shall I go from thy Spirit?
> Or whither shall I flee from thy presence?
> If I ascend to heaven, thou art there!
> If I make my bed in Sheōl, thou art there!
> (Ps. cxxxix.7f)

And when Israel's heroic age returned once more, in the days of the Maccabees, and men flung away their lives in defence of their faith, their sanctuary, and their sacred Law, then the conviction arose that God, being just, could not allow these heroes, these martyrs for His own cause, to lie down in the dust forever—or their souls to flit like birds in the dim halls of Sheōl. "And many of those who sleep in the dust of the earth shall awake, some to everlasting life, and some to shame and everlasting contempt" (Dan. xii.2). This was as natural and necessary a conclusion for faith as it was later to be for the author of the Apocalypse of John. And it was phrased in terms of a bodily resurrection for the simple reason that, under the influence of the Persian religion, during two long centuries, the Jews had come to think of resurrection as the normal mode of restoration, and the survival of a disembodied spirit as something much less adequate.

On the other hand, as we have seen (p. 33), Alexandrian Jews who were familiar with Greek philosophy, especially that of Plato, tended to think of the redeemed or divinely rescued soul as "safe in the hand of God," and "at peace."

> For though in the sight of men they were punished,
> their hope is full of immortality.

Having been disciplined a little, they will receive great
good,
because God tested them and found them worthy of
himself. (Wis. III.4-5)

Now the most notable thing about both these types of
faith in a life to come is that there is no suggestion that the
soul is by nature immortal (though the author of the Book
of Wisdom clearly believed that God originally intended
man to be immortal: see Wis. II.23f). Instead, the life to
come is God's gift to those who are worthy. Plato and
other philosophers had tried to find support for the idea
of the soul's immortality. For example, the phenomenon
of motion, which either continues indefinitely or imparts
its force to some other body (as Newton also recognised);
or the logical theory of causation, which can work backward as well as forward, and prove the pre-existence as
well as the survival of the soul, the *psychē* or individual
life-force—both these arguments seemed to favour the
natural immortality of the soul, but neither of them is
even considered in the Bible. Here, as wherever eternal
life is a matter of faith and not of speculation, and especially when martyrdom has set a serious problem for religion, the conviction rests upon the goodness, the justice,
the mercy and love of *God*, not the nature of man's soul.

And the same is true of Paul, and of the whole New
Testament. True, Paul speaks of the resurrection of "the
body," not the flesh (for Paul, "flesh" was more or less
abhorrent, as it was the seat of sin with its hopeless infection and corruption); but he does not mean the body
that is buried in the grave. Instead, "the body which is
to be" is given by God (I Cor. xv.35-38), and will be incorruptible, powerful, glorious, and imperishable—for
"flesh and blood cannot inherit the kingdom of God, nor
does the perishable inherit the imperishable" (I Cor. xv.
40-50). This new and glorified body must be "put on" at
the resurrection. Paul shudders at the thought of a bare,

naked, purely "spiritual" (as we would say, but he would say "psychic") existence, that of a disembodied soul: "not that we would be unclothed, but that we would be further clothed [or reclothed], so that what is mortal may be swallowed up by life. . . ." And yet he goes on to say: "we would rather be away from the body and at home with the Lord" (II Cor. v.1-10; cf. Phil. 1.19-26). Of course Paul is not writing a treatise on Systematic Theology—his letters are more like sermons. But the occasional chance-phrase is as clearly an expression of his real convictions as are the formal statements. For example in I Cor. v.3-5, he directs his readers to hold a church court and try the man who is guilty of incest (so the case was viewed in both Jewish and Roman law): "you are to deliver this man to Satan for the destruction of the flesh, that his *spirit* may be saved in the day of the Lord Jesus." In this passage there is no reference to any resurrection of the body; though Paul certainly expected the man to die (by Satan's action) after he was excommunicated—the words provided a terrible text for the later Inquisition! Evidently Paul was concerned for the saving of the man's "spirit", not the resurrection of his "body". And there are other passages which likewise indicate that Paul, instead of championing the traditional Palestinian-Pharisaic doctrine of resurrection against the Hellenistic-philosophical view of immortality, in effect combines the two—as he often does, and as all powerful, creative religious thinkers tend to do—bringing forth out of their treasures "what is new and what is old" (Mt. XIII.52).

Today, we are "caught betwixt two"—the naturalistic view which bids us live the noblest life we can, regardless of any life to come:

Hath man no second life? Pitch this one high!

and the religious view for which it is all but inconceivable that God, who is supremely good, just, and loving, should allow those who serve Him utterly and lay down their lives in His service, to perish and "be as if they had never been". It is not a matter of speculation or of probability or of the accumulating psychical evidence for "survival of bodily death"; it is purely a matter of *faith*. And if we really do know God—i.e. if the religious life is based upon valid experience and not illusion—then we cannot view it as a matter of indifference whether or not we ourselves— and, even more important, those whom we love—survive and "enter into the joy of their Lord", free from the limitations, the burdens, and the frustrations of this mortal life, and also free from sinning. For love, God's love, "never ends. . . . For now we see in a mirror dimly, but then face to face. Now I know in part; then I shall understand fully, even as I have been fully understood" (1 Cor. XIII.8-12). As in the Book of Revelation, as in the frescos and mosaics of the ancient Christian churches, as even in some of the wall-paintings in the catacombs, the martyrs, who have "loved not their lives unto death" are celebrated as victors with Christ. And in the Church's ancient hymns they are described as throned with Him in glory:

> Now they sit in heavenly places,
> Now they reign with Christ their king.

(See Lk. XXII.28-30; 1 Cor. VI.3; Rev. III.21.) This has nothing to do with resurrection. If the picture is true at all, it is true *now*, as well as on the Day of Judgment. And in spite of all the interesting variations upon the theme, in creeds, in hymns and liturgies, in theology and church art, this conviction—namely that the winners are *already* crowned—has always been among the most basic of Christian beliefs.

For Further Reading

I. CHRISTIANITY AND OTHER RELIGIONS

A. C. BOUQUET, *The Christian Faith and Non-Christian Religions*. London 1959.

F. C. GRANT, *Hellenistic Religions*. New York 1953.

— *Ancient Roman Religion*. New York 1957.

R. E. HUME, *The World's Living Religions*. Edinburgh and New York 1955.

E. O. JAMES, *The History of Religions*. London 1956.

A. JEFFERY, *Islam*. New York 1958.

N. MICKLEM, *Religion*. Oxford and New York 1948.

M. P. NILSSON, *History of Greek Religion*. Oxford and New York 1925 (new ed., 1949).

— *Greek Piety*, id., 1948.

W. R. SMITH, *The Religion of the Semites*, 2nd ed. London 1894 (new ed., paperback, New York 1957).

II. BELIEF IN GOD

(a) *The Bible*

E. C. COLWELL, *The Study of the Bible*. Chicago 1937.

C. H. DODD, *The Authority of the Bible*. London and New York 1928.

H. E. FOSDICK, *A Guide to Understanding the Bible*. New York 1938.

R. M. GRANT, *The Bible in the Church*. New York 1948; rev. ed. 1954.

F. KENYON, *The Story of the Bible*. London 1947.

J. KNOX, *Criticism and Faith*. London and New York 1952.

T. W. MANSON, *A Companion to the Bible*. Edinburgh and New York 1939.

I. M. PRICE, *The Ancestry of our English Bible*, new ed. New York 1949.

H. H. ROWLEY, *The Relevance of the Bible*. London and New York 1942.

(b) *Religion of the Old Testament*

M. BURROWS, *An Outline of Biblical Theology*. Philadelphia 1946.

J. MUILENBURG, "History of the Religion of Israel", in *The Interpreter's Bible*, Vol. I, pp. 292-348. New York 1952.

J. PEDERSEN, *Israel, its life and culture*, 2 Vols. Oxford and New York 1926, 1940.

H. W. Robinson, *Inspiration and Revelation in the Old Testament.* Oxford and New York 1946.
— *Religious Ideas of the Old Testament.* New York and London 1913, reprint 1952.
J. Skinner, *Prophecy and Religion.* Cambridge and New York 1922.
A. C. Welch, *Religion of Israel under the Kingdom.* Edinburgh 1912.
G. E. Wright, "The Faith of Israel", in *The Interpreter's Bible,* Vol. I, pp. 349-389. New York 1952.

(c) *The New Testament*

R. Bultmann, *Theology of the New Testament,* 2 Vols. London and New York 1951, 1952.
F. C. Grant, *Introduction to New Testament Thought.* New York 1950.
— *Ancient Judaism and the New Testament.* New York 1959; Edinburgh 1960.
G. F. Moore, *Judaism in the First Centuries of the Christian Era,* 3 Vols. Oxford and Harvard 1927-30.
H. F. Rall, *Religion as Salvation.* London and New York 1953.
C. C. Richardson, *The Doctrine of the Trinity.* New York 1958.

III. Sin and Forgiveness

O. Baab, *Theology of the Old Testament.* New York 1949.
A. B. Davidson, *Theology of the Old Testament.* Edinburgh and New York 1907.
F. C. Grant, *How to Read the Bible* (esp. Ch. III). New York 1956, Edinburgh 1959.
— *The Epistle to the Hebrews.* New York 1956.
G. B. Gray, *Sacrifice in the Old Testament.* Oxford and New York 1925.
J. Muilenburg, G. E. Wright, and W. R. Smith, as above.

IV. Belief in Christ
(a) *Jesus*

G. Bornkamm, *Jesus von Nazareth.* Stuttgart 1956 (3rd ed. 1959).
B. H. Branscomb, *Jesus and the Law of Moses.* New York 1930.
M. Dibelius, *Jesus.* Philadelphia 1949.
S. M. Gilmour, *The Gospel Jesus Preached.* New York 1957.
F. C. Grant, *The Gospel of the Kingdom.* New York 1940.
S. E. Johnson, *Jesus in this Homeland.* New York and London, 1958.
T. W. Manson, *The Sayings of Jesus.* London 1949.
C. C. McCown, *The Search for the Real Jesus.* New York 1940.
H. Windisch, *The Meaning of the Sermon on the Mount.* Philadelphia 1951.

(b) *Paul*

H. B. CARRÉ, *Paul's Doctrine of Redemption*. New York 1914.

A. DEISSMANN, *Paul*, 2nd ed. London 1926 (reprint, New York 1957).

M. DIBELIUS, *St. Paul*. London and New York 1953.

W. L. KNOX, *St. Paul and the Church of the Gentiles*. Cambridge and New York 1939.

A. D. NOCK, *St. Paul*. Oxford and New York 1937.

H. F. RALL, *According to Paul*. New York 1944.

(c) *Christology*

J. KNOX, *Jesus Lord and Christ*. New York 1958.

— *The Death of Christ*. New York 1958.

C. M. LAYMON, *Christ in the New Testament*. New York 1958.

W. NORMAN PITTENGER, *The Word Incarnate*. London 1959.

V. TAYLOR, *Names of Jesus*. London and New York 1953.

A. N. WILDER, *New Testament Faith for Today*. New York 1955.

(d) *The Creeds*

J. N. D. KELLY, *Early Christian Creeds*. London and New York 1950.

See also the commentaries on the New Testament in *The Interpreter's Bible*, Vols. VII-XII.

V. THE HOLY SPIRIT AND THE CHURCH

E. BEVAN, *Christianity*. Oxford and New York 1932.

R. M. GRANT, *Gnosticism and Early Christianity*. Oxford and New York 1959.

J. N. D. KELLY, *Early Christian Doctrines*. London 1958.

H. A. A. KENNEDY, *The Theology of the Epistles*. London and New York 1919.

H. LIETZMANN, *The Beginnings of the Christian Church*, vol I. New York 1938.

H. W. ROBINSON, *Christian Experience of the Holy Spirit*. New York and London 1928.

E. F. SCOTT, *The Spirit in the New Testament*. London 1923.

J. WEISS, *History of Primitive Christianity*, 2 Vols. New York 1937; new ed. as paperback 1959.

VI. THE LIFE OF THE WORLD TO COME

J. BAILLIE, *And the Life Everlasting*. New York and Oxford 1950.

E. BEVAN, *The Hope of the World to Come*. London 1930.

F. CUMONT, *After Life in Roman Paganism*. New Haven 1922.

J. DENNEY, *Factors of Faith in Immortality*. London 1910.

L. R. FARNELL, *Greek Hero Cults and Ideas of Immortality*. Oxford and New York 1921.

F. V. Filson, *Jesus Christ the Risen Lord*. New York 1956.

H. E. Fosdick, *The Assurance of Immortality*. New York 1913.

F. C. Grant, *Can we still Believe in Immortality?* Louisville 1946.

R. M. Grant, *The Sword and the Cross*. New York 1955.

A. S. Pringle-Pattison, *The Idea of Immortality*. New York and Oxford 1922.

B. H. Streeter, ed., *Immortality*. New York 1925.

F. von Hügel, *Eternal Life*. Edinburgh 1912.